BAJC

AUG -- 2017

NATIONAL GEOGRAPHIC KiDS

125 Pet Rescues

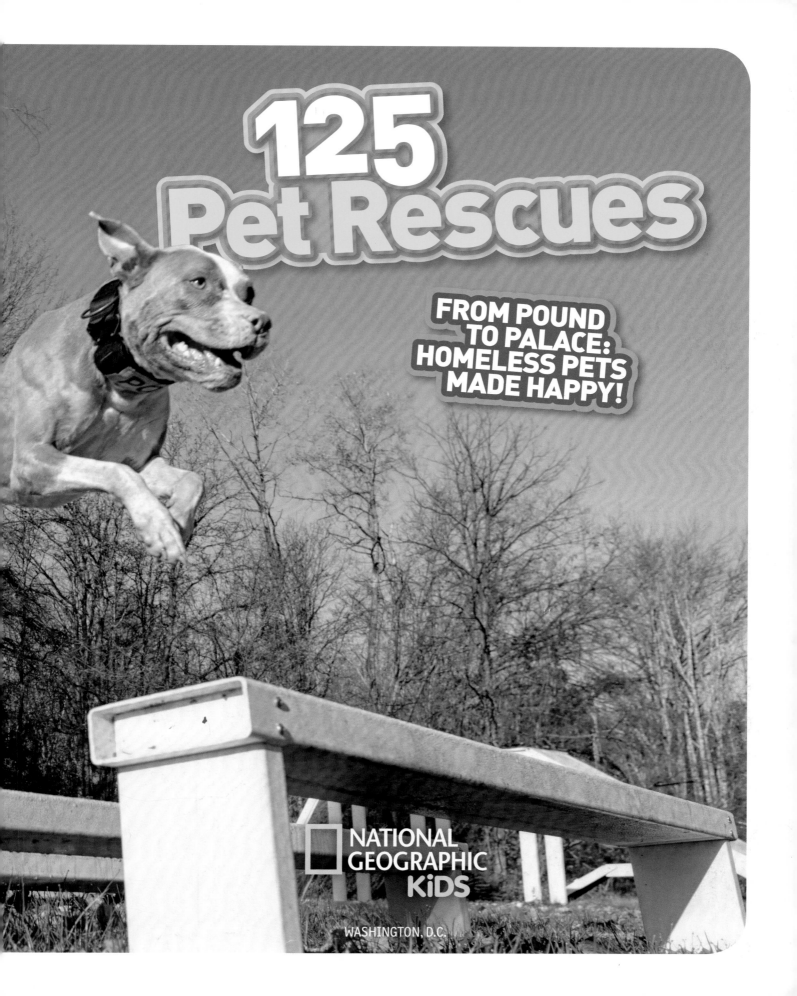

125 Pet Rescues

FROM POUND TO PALACE: HOMELESS PETS MADE HAPPY!

NATIONAL
GEOGRAPHIC
KiDS

WASHINGTON, D.C.

Contents

5

Foreword

Best Friends Animal Society

WELCOME! You're about to meet some incredible animals who have had some amazing adventures.

In many ways, they're just like the pets in your own life. They have their quirks, they're adorable, each one is different, and yet they all just want to be loved. These animals didn't start off with happy families who cared for them, though. They had to go on long and sometimes harrowing journeys to find happily-ever-afters.

In fact, there are millions of pets like these all across the country who are looking for homes. You can find them in animal shelters or at rescue groups. Sometimes, you might even see them as strays, wandering the streets alone. Adopting one is a tremendous act of love. No matter where they come from or what they look like, every one of them deserves a friend. I hope the next time you're looking for a pet, you'll adopt one who really needs you.

But even if you're not ready for a new pet, there are so many ways that you can help. You can bring toys or blankets to animals waiting for homes. You can think of ways to raise money for them. Or you can show photos of animals at the shelter to all of your friends and neighbors.

Homeless pets need everyone's help.

Long ago, my friends and I set out to help pets like these. In fact, we went so far as to buy a big piece of land out in the

Justin
Page 48

King O.
Page 49

canyons of Utah. We decided to make it a safe place for animals who didn't have anywhere else to go. And now, around 1,700 animals live there on any given day! Some are dogs, some are cats, some are horses, some are bunny rabbits, some are parrots, some are goats, and some are even pet pigs. All of them live happily here while they wait for families to come adopt them. You can visit us anytime you like! It's called Best Friends Animal Sanctuary, and some say it's the most beautiful (and most loving) place on Earth.

But it takes more than one sanctuary to help all of the pets. That's why Best Friends also has programs to help animals all across the country. And that's why the animals need friends like you, too.

So please enjoy these stories of love, laughter, and unforgettable pets. Carry these tales in your heart. And remember them the next time you see an animal—or a person—who could use an act of kindness. Kindness is a powerful force. Every time we use it, we change a little piece of the world for the better. And every time we use it, it changes us for the better, too. The kinder we are, the richer our lives become.

And what better to inspire kindness than a precious animal? So let the reading begin ...
Enjoy!

*Best Friends
co-founder and CEO*
Gregory Castle

Roosevelt
Page 49

Introduction

WELCOME TO THE fantastic, funny, and heartwarming world of rescued pets. Paw, pad, hop, or clip-clop through these pages to find 125 of National Geographic Kids' favorite true tales of kindness, survival, pampering, love, and more. Meet an orphaned duck who gets regular pedicures, a rescued cat who saved his owner's life just hours after adoption, and a dog brought home on a private jet. Oh, and don't forget about the little frozen piglet who was pulled out of a snowbank and now lives a life of luxury.

Most of these happy endings wouldn't have been possible without the dedicated shelter staff, rescue workers, and volunteers working hard on and off duty to make life sweeter for animals in need. These people work at adoption events, fund-raise, foster, or make time to come and walk the shelter dogs or brush and play with the cats.

They also rescue, rehabilitate, nurture, and rehome scared and sometimes injured animals who have been abused. How could anyone hurt an animal? It's not an easy question to answer, but abuse does happen. Fortunately, there are many hardworking animal lovers out there trying to make the world a better place for animals, one beloved pet at a time.

These delightful stories are not only fun to read, they are important. Rescue animals need our help. Homeless horses, cats, dogs, and other animals lose their homes when their owners can't care for them anymore for whatever reason. They need voices to speak on their behalf. They need homes! Even if you can't adopt an animal, you can read about them and help get the word out about amazing, adoptable animals. So flip the page, let the fur fly, and join this party of precious rescued pets.

Super Teddy
Page 38

Little Squeak
Page 14

Lil Bub
Page 98

Mocha
Page 54

KULI
Page 34

LURLENE AND NOLAND

THANKS, MOM!

WHERE: CLEVELAND, OHIO, U.S.A.

At the Cleveland Animal Protective League, a heroic young mother cat raised an abandoned pit bull mix puppy like he was one of her own kittens. When he first arrived, the sad day-old puppy was in bad shape and didn't have much of a hope of survival without his mother. That's when his caregivers took a chance and added him to a pile of newborn kittens snuggled up with their young mother, Lurlene. This maternal sweetie took the tiny orphaned puppy under her paw. With a nuzzle and a lick, she treated him like her own. When caregivers took Noland away for extra meals, Lurlene kept an eye on their every move to make sure her pup was safe. Noland grew healthy and strong. When he was old enough, he was adopted into a wonderful forever home. And sweet Lurlene doesn't have to work so hard anymore. She's been adopted into a wonderful home, too. Now *she* gets taken care of 24/7. Meow!

CADENCE

WHERE: LOS ANGELES, CALIFORNIA, U.S.A.

When her rescuers approached, the scared pit bull cowered, her eyes swollen with painful cuts and scrapes. From the dark alley, she looked up with fear but also a glimmer of hope. Named Cadence by her rescuers, this sweet pup is believed to have been used for dog fighting. This cruel and illegal sport pits two fighting dogs against one another for human entertainment. Sometimes timid dogs like Cadence are used as practice targets for fighting dogs. Sweet, scared, and in pain, this sad dog went willingly with the heroes trying to save her. Back at the rescue called Hope for Paws, she received medical care, food, and a safe and comfortable place to sleep. Within a day, the gentle pup snuggled and smooched her adoring caregivers. But Cadence still had a challenge ahead. When she was well enough, she had eye surgery to save her sight. Fully recuperated, it wasn't too long before Cadence was adopted into a loving home. Now she lives like a queen! Her family refers to her as "The Lady" of the house. She also gets unlimited belly rubs.

AJ NUGGET

WHERE: FT. LAUDERDALE, FLORIDA, U.S.A.

Like many racehorses who don't win at the track, AJ Nugget found himself without a home. He was injured and hungry. A group of Good Samaritans bought the colt and sent him to Pure Thoughts Horse Rescue. He was in such bad shape, no one knew if he would survive the trip. AJ also had to learn to trust humans again after being so badly mistreated. But he felt safe with his rescuers and soon began to relax and heal. A volunteer at the rescue named Martha Bouza donated money for AJ's care. She helped tend to his wounds. The following year, when AJ was healthy, happy, and ready to be adopted, Martha couldn't part with the handsome horse who had caught her eye and won her heart. Now AJ lives life like a king. He has a big paddock, friends, and loads of fresh hay to snack on. He gets regular exercise and has even won a blue ribbon at a horse show. One thing is for sure: This horse is a winner, no matter what.

BEFORE

AFTER

Horses gallop at around 27 miles an hour (44 km/h).

13

LITTLE SQUEAK

WHERE: VICTORIA, AUSTRALIA

This little piggy has a serious job at the sanctuary where she lives: CHO, or Chief Happiness Officer. When staff members arrive each day at Edgar's Mission, Squeak greets them with the joyful "squeak" she was named for. She never fails to put a smile on her humans' faces. Squeak was surrendered to an animal shelter at just two months old when her owner could no longer care for her. Her name is Little Squeak, but she's got a big personality. She loves oinking away at her best dog friend, eating watermelon, and getting into messes! She also loves belly rubs and mud baths to keep cool. This little cutie will live out her days romping with friends and eating carrots and apples till her heart is content at the sanctuary for lucky farm animals.

CHIEF HAPPINESS OFFICER, REPORTING FOR DUTY!

NATE

WHERE: SEAL BEACH, CALIFORNIA, U.S.A.

Nate the husky had a hard start in life. Until he was two years old, he had been used as a research animal in a laboratory. That means he probably had to endure medical testing. Somehow he got out, escaped, or was abandoned. Shelter workers from Seal Beach Animal Care Center found him wandering the streets, and cared for the scared, injured dog. Then the Beagle Freedom Project, which helps rehabilitate laboratory dogs, took Nate in. Nervous Nate was loved, socialized, trained, and given a chance to trust humans again. It wasn't long before his goofy personality emerged. He loved to play and run, especially with other friendly dogs. When he finished his rehabilitation, Nate joined a foster home. But the real question was: Would he find a forever home? Yes! Now Nate is living in a happy home with two other big dogs and lots of freedom, belly rubs, and good meals.

Huskies' thick double coats keep them warm.

HAMILTON

WHERE: SAN JOSE, CALIFORNIA, U.S.A.

This cool cat was born a stray. He was a feral cat, which is a domesticated cat left to fend for himself outside. He was picked up by a caring human and brought into the Humane Society of Silicon Valley. Volunteers set out to socialize the skittish kitten, whom they named Hamilton, to increase his chances of being adopted. It's not easy to convince a scared, hissing kitty (even one with a marvelous milky mustache) to trust humans. But young Hammy decided to give it a try. Little by little, he bonded with his new owner. He did hide in the bathroom for a while, but then graduated to a cozy closet. As he became more trusting of his environment, little Ham took over the whole house! Meanwhile, his new owner loved to snap pictures of the kitty's unusual face. These days, when this cat's not hamming it up in front of the camera, he's doing what cats do: playing, sleeping, and spying. He and his family also advocate for animal shelters. Hamilton is the cat's meow!

PERFECT PIT BULLS

Precious pit bulls can make perfect pets, but these delightful blocky-headed dogs are often overlooked at animal rescues for fear that they'll be aggressive. But don't judge these books by their covers—these gentle souls will melt your heart in a minute.

"Pit bull" does not refer to one dog breed. It is a name often used to describe several breeds of dogs with similar features and characteristics.

BRUTUS

WHERE: ARLINGTON, VIRGINIA, U.S.A.

When a young couple adopted a six-month-old pit bull mix from the Washington Humane Society in Washington, D.C., he'd been there for months and not a single person had considered adopting him. But he didn't let the long, lonely days get him down. In all that time, Brutus never showed an ounce of aggression or grouchiness to dogs or people. This sunshiny guy was all puppy love and big brown eyes—and loads of potential.

In his new home, Brutus's owners put the youngster on a strict regimen of love, training, socialization, and snuggles. Brutus grew up to be a perfect gentleman, though his behavior is subject to goofy bouts of silliness. He loves to throw down some fun at the dog park. Brutus also has tons of affection for his humans and favorite playmate, his family's tiny, senior shih tzu mix, Shisha. He couldn't be more gentle with her. His overwhelmingly good nature has even rubbed off on his sister, who in the past had been a bit snarly with other dogs. But with Brutus's good influence, even Shisha has cleaned up her act. She's being much nicer to other dogs these days thanks to her big brother, Bru.

CHERRY

WHERE: ENFIELD, CONNECTICUT, U.S.A.

When a tenderhearted pit bull named Cherry was rescued from a fighting ring, he was so guarded and scared, his rescuers at Best Friends Animal Society in Utah didn't have many clues about his real personality. When a potential adopter came along, he had a well-socialized pit bull mix named Madison who he believed could be a great mentor and healer for Cherry. However, Cherry had just had knee surgery at the rescue and wasn't anywhere near ready to be adopted. But these humans were determined. They followed the strict adoption guidelines and followed the dog's progress in rehab. Finally, after months of waiting, the potential adopters—including Madison—were invited to meet Cherry. It took about an hour before Cherry would come out and begin to trust his new family, but he chose Madison first. After about three weeks he began to settle in, with Madison as his supportive mama. His humans slept in the same bed with him so he'd feel safe. Now he travels with his family to teach others about the wonders of pit bulls. But his all-time favorite thing to do? Cuddle. This shining star has a heart of gold.

Cherry loves to sit (or snuggle) in people's laps.

FIONA AND BRODY HIPPO

Brody can speak and even whisper on command.

WHERE: SOUTH CAROLINA, U.S.A.

FIONA

BRODY

Meeting him for the first time, you might mistake Brody for a hippo instead of a dog! This chunky hunk of love adores his "hippo lifestyle," and spends his time wallowing in cool mud holes. But this handsome hound's life hasn't always been so happy. When his loving parents first met him, Brody had been abandoned by his previous owner in a basement. Luckily, dog lovers Stephen and Van took quick action and brought the scared pup home to live with them. Right away, Brody adored his new life, but still, something was missing ... a hippo sister! Thanks to a rescue called Change of Heart Pit Bull Rescue, a beautiful little dog named Fiona had been saved from a bad situation. She was covered in scabs, and nearly bald from a mite infestation. But when Stephen and Van saw her, they knew she was perfect. Just like Brody, the stocky girl loved to cuddle, give gentle kisses, and even make happy little grunts like a real hippo. Now happily living with their forever family, these two pit bull mixes spend their time playing, snuggling, and hamming it up for their fans on social media. They also act as advocates for pit bulls and other needy dogs, showing just how wonderful adopting can be. Good hippos—er, dogs!

WHERE: OAKTON, VIRGINIA, U.S.A.

When an 11-year-old girl named Julia saw children on a farm playing too rough with a helpless kitten, she took action. With permission from the farm's owner and help from her family, she rounded up the whole litter of flea-infested tabbies. Her aunt put in a call to the Feline Foundation of Greater Washington, in Washington, D.C. The rescue group offered to take the kittens. After a visit to the vet and a soothing, soaking flea bath, the kittens thrived in their comfy foster home. Meanwhile, Julia convinced her parents to adopt one of the kittens. She picked the cute brown tabby, brought him home, named him Harley, and has been devoted to him ever since. For 15 years, Harley's life has been nonstop kisses, catnip, and canned food. Wherever Julia goes, this adorable love bug is sure to follow.

HARLEY

DID YOU SAY "TUNA"?

ABBEY AND ZEUS

I HOPE THE WEDDING CAKE IS BEEF-FLAVORED!

WHERE: MECHANICSBURG, PENNSYLVANIA, U.S.A.

This inseparable pair met at the Speranza Animal Rescue, where they both landed with separate but serious life stories of abuse. Shy Abbey spent more than two years waiting for the right family, but her shyness was a barrier to adoption. That changed when Zeus came along. He was bruised and missing an eye and also extremely shy. Meeting each other was a pivotal moment. Once they had each other, they became inseparable, and their confidence grew in leaps and bounds. They seemed to make each other feel safe.

Miraculously, a couple offered to adopt them as a pair. Before they left for their new home, the shelter hosted a wedding for the canine couple. The dogs dressed up in their finest attire for the formal outdoor ceremony, an officiant read wedding vows, and the dogs exchanged new collars (instead of rings). After reading their wedding vows, the officiant declared the pair husband and wife, telling Zeus, "You may now lick your bride."

PEACHES

WHERE: CHARLOTTE, NORTH CAROLINA, U.S.A.

Peaches the pit bull suffered in an abusive home, was scheduled to be euthanized in a shelter (this is when animals are humanely put to death, usually due to overcrowding in shelters), and later survived cancer. But then she got adopted. Her new owner saw a sparkle in her eye. She invested in her dog with training, time, and love. Sweet, gentle, and smart, Peaches passed her therapy dog certification test with ease. She traveled with her owner to schools and nursing homes to inspire those in need, and all over the country to provide comfort to people in the aftermath of disasters. The American Pit Bull Foundation even recognized Peaches's hard work by making her a mascot. Her job was to help spread awareness about how pit bulls can be great dogs and do good in the world. She posed for pictures (sometimes wearing a tutu or bunny ears) and spread cheer to everyone she met. Sadly, Peaches passed away in the spring of 2016 after another battle with cancer. But her legacy lives on in dedicated and do-gooding pit bulls everywhere.

19

ELLE

Elle knows a command for "stop, drop, and roll" to help firefighters teach kids what to do if their clothes catch on fire.

I PUT THE "MODEL" IN "ROLE MODEL"!

WHERE: ROANOKE RAPIDS, NORTH CAROLINA, U.S.A.

This rescued pit bull beauty almost spent her life being made to have puppies just so her owners could sell them. But when she got a second chance for a better future, this bighearted dog decided to take a bite out of life. With training, love, and care from her new owner, Leah Brewer, Elle has transformed into a beloved therapy dog. She helps elementary school kids practice reading to build confidence. She also gives them a lot of comfort when they get stressed out by schoolwork. She's calm, patient, supportive, and exudes unconditional love. With help from Leah, Elle even started a reading program called Tail Wagging Tales. And in 2013, she was named the American Hero Dog by the American Humane Association! When she's not working, this hero loves to hike, swim, and play with her canine brother, Bruno. She even loves to watch TV and is known to hog the comfiest recliner in the house. Read on, Elle!

Dogs have been living with humans for at least 14,000 years.

MARNIE

Marnie's favorite foods include watermelon, chicken, and broccoli.

WHERE: NEW YORK, NEW YORK, U.S.A.

Click! Click! Click! Marnie might be a top dog model now, but this photogenic phenom was originally left on the street to fend for herself. The senior shih tzu was found stinky and covered in matted hair by an animal control officer. Her rescuers delivered her to a shelter. Caregivers named the 10-year-old hot mess Stinky. She had an unusual but endearing permanent head tilt, which won the heart of her new owner, who renamed her Marnie. After some serious dental work, the little stinker started to smell like a flower. Marnie's owner took her to parties and on long walks. She also took a lot of pictures. It wasn't long before just about everyone on the Internet (well, nearly two million people, anyway) followed Marnie's photographic journey on social media channels. These days, in addition to posing for the camera, Marvelous Marnie loves running and exploring and snacking with her BFFs. She still doesn't love baths, but she does enjoy primping and getting dressed up in sweaters, hats, and all kinds of costumes to pose for pics and please her adoring fans.

BIG MIKE

WHERE: EGG HARBOR TOWNSHIP, NEW JERSEY, U.S.A.

Big Mike was a huge, 20-pound (9-kg) homeless cat roaming the neighborhood. Because of his beefy size, people thought the stray was a bullying brute. But one day, Big Mike was seen looking out for a little neighborhood cat named Stoney, who was on his way home. Some other cats beat up on Stoney. Big Mike didn't like that one bit. He used his size to his advantage, getting between Stoney and the other cats, then escorted the little cat home. After that, Stoney and Big Mike became friends. It wasn't long before Stoney's human family adopted Big Mike. After that, Big Mike had his own home, and Stoney had his own guard cat.

STONEY

MIKE

Mike may be big, but the largest domestic cat breed is the Maine coon.

CAITLYN

WHERE: CHARLESTON, SOUTH CAROLINA, U.S.A.

This girl made big headlines after being found abandoned with her muzzle taped shut. She was unable to eat or to drink water. No one knows why someone would do something so cruel to an animal. But it didn't stop the dog from wanting to give her rescuers cuddles and love. Caretakers at the Charleston Animal Society named the sweet dog Caitlyn and did everything they could to help her, including reconstructive surgery to fix her injured jaw and tongue. Now that she's all healed, the busy girl serves as an ambassador for all rescue dogs. A true superdog, she helps raise money for rescue animals by posing for photos for fund-raisers, attending events in a superhero costume, and going on media "interviews." The famous Fido makes a great ambassa-*dog*—spreading wags and barks about the importance of animal rescue and her own amazing ability to forgive, forget, and just have fun.

BEFORE

AFTER

JUSTIN

MONTCLAIR, NEW JERSEY, U.S.A.

Justin the kitten lost his ears to severe burns and suffered badly burned skin on his head and back. Thankfully, he made a full recovery. He had help from the kind person who saved him, the Animal Alliance of New Jersey, and Crown Veterinary Specialists. Now in his forever home, Justin never lets his old injuries get in the way of a good life—his family dotes on him and calls him "earless and fearless." Justin has a social media page, where his more than 100,000 fans can follow his catnip parties and his own special "boot camp" for the foster kitties he helps his owner care for. Thanks to social media, now Justin's a magnet for helping others raise money for animals in need. His page has helped raise more than $35,000 for shelters and homeless animals. There's no doubt about it, this lucky cat is paying it forward, one pawful of pennies at a time.

The "tuxedo" pattern can occur on almost any kind of domestic cat.

DAISY

WHERE: **RIO RANCHO, NEW MEXICO, U.S.A.**

Petite and perfect but very shy, Daisy the dwarf hamster lost her home and ended up at a rescue called Haven for Hamsters. Daisy was quiet, almost always hiding in her little house when potential adopters visited. Her caregiver figured she'd live out her days at the rescue. But Daisy had other ideas. One day, the family Daisy had been waiting for walked through the door. She dashed out of her house and squeaked. She let them hold her and play with her. After that day, Daisy was never homeless again.

DAISY IS A DWARF HAMSTER LIKE THE ONES PICTURED HERE.

Dwarf hamsters are the smallest breed of hamster.

WALLACE

WHERE: **WASHINGTON, D.C., U.S.A.**

Sometimes, animals have a lot to teach us about getting through hard times. As an older kitten, this sweet babe was found scavenging for food on the street with a broken leg. Cat lover Courtney Hunt noticed the kitten and knew he needed medical care. She took the dirty, shy, and scared kitten to a vet, who said the cat's leg would require amputation. Within hours of his surgery, the little cat was hobbling around like nothing had ever happened. For her birthday, Courtney asked her friends for donations to help care for the little cat, whom she had named Wallace. And for the best gift of all: a friend named Marcella Fredriksson adopted Wallace. Now he has a wonderful life with lots of fun and love. These days he loves bird-watching from the window of his apartment, jumping in empty boxes, chasing string, and sitting on crinkly paper. He also loves a good eyebrow massage and, even though this loyal and kind kitty only has three legs, he has no problem running around the house and flying off the furniture. From down on his luck to living the high life, Wallace is truly an inspiration.

FANTASTIC FRIENDSHIPS

Some rescued pets show us how good things can come out of bad situations—like new friends or a reunion with someone we love. These special sweeties show us the true meaning of friendship.

Guinea pigs purr when they are content.

HERNANDO CORTÉS AND MONTEZUMA

WHERE: VICTORIA, AUSTRALIA

One day, these two tricolor pocket pets were discovered outdoors after having been abandoned. They had dodged scary traffic and—even more frightening—loose dogs until a Good Samaritan bundled them up and brought them to a nearby vet clinic. The quivering guinea pigs stuck to each other like glue. Once they were safe at the clinic, a vet checked them out and delivered them to a nearby animal rescue organization called Edgar's Mission. This very bonded pair is currently living out a fairy-tale life together at the sanctuary, where they cuddle and nest in a cute little castle, gobble their favorite treat (tomatoes), and skip on their exercise wheel on a daily basis.

TULAH AND BUMBLE

WHERE: MALIBU, CALIFORNIA, U.S.A.

Many people expect big dogs to be fearless. But for Tulah, a mixed breed rescued from wandering the streets, life was scary. She loved her new humans, but was timid and spent most of her time shyly curled up in an armchair. Then her new family adopted another rescue dog. Bumble the mastiff mix was even bigger than Tulah, but also more frightened! He had come into the shelter with bruises, a broken leg that hadn't healed quite right, and kennel cough. When he got to his new home, Bumble was too scared to wag his tail, and didn't know how to go up or down stairs. But lucky for this petrified pup, something amazing happened—timid Tulah took him under her paw. Bumble gave Tulah the courage she hadn't had before. Tulah drew Bumble out of his shell with games of doggie tag, cuddled with him at night, and taught him to use the stairs. She even shared her toys and treats with him. These days, the inseparable pair spends their time romping, playing, and cuddling. These two are big dogs with even bigger hearts!

TULAH

BUMBLE

Some breeds of mastiff can weigh up to 200 pounds (90 kg).

MR. G AND JELLYBEAN

I'M SWEET ON YOU, JELLYBEAN!

WHERE: GRASS VALLEY, CALIFORNIA, U.S.A.

Mr. G was the saddest goat around. He had been rescued from a neglectful home and relocated to a 600-acre (243-ha) sanctuary called Animal Place. Mr. G was safe, but he wasn't happy. He wouldn't eat or leave the corner of his stall. For six days, his caregivers worried he was sick. But the vet said the goat was depressed. Was he missing his longtime pal, a small donkey named Jellybean? The pair had lived together for 10 years in a cramped, hot paddock with no shade and little food or water. After their rescue, Jellybean had been relocated to a different sanctuary.

Mr. G's caregivers would do just about anything to cheer up the old goat. They searched for and found Jellybean, and offered to give him a home. Then a volunteer drove 14 hours to pick him up. When Jellybean stepped off the horse trailer, Mr. G's ears perked up. His nostrils quivered. He stood up for the first time in days. Then he took a few cautious steps toward his furry, long-eared friend. It wasn't long before Mr. G was happy and eating. Now these BFFs are inseparable again. The sanctuary has promised to keep the pair together for life.

TONY D.

WHERE: MORENO VALLEY, CALIFORNIA, U.S.A.

When Tony D.'s owner suffered serious health problems and lost her job, she asked the Kentucky Equine Humane Center for help. Could they help find a new home for her beloved horse? The kind rescuers took Tony in, even though he needed a special diet to keep him healthy. A few months later, the stars aligned for Tony D. when a family in California wanted to adopt him. The family's horse-loving daughter was a perfect match for Tony: She was also on a special diet because of a medical condition. Soon the horse made a cross-country trek in a horse van. In California, Tony D. has a great new life— he lives on a ranch with other horses, llamas, and doting humans. Twice a day his family serves him specially prepared meals. His new owner has also discovered all the places where Tony likes a good scratch (like between his spotted ears).

TEDDY

WHERE: LIVONIA, NEW YORK, U.S.A.

This rescue dog followed his nose and his instincts to save his family's life during a dangerous house fire. The blaze was just starting to crackle and burn that night when the doggie do-gooder bounded upstairs to alert his owner, who ran downstairs to find flames engulfing the living room ceiling. She grabbed her kids and everyone ran to safety without a minute to spare. The family had rescued Teddy a year before when they found him starving and alone in a park. Though they lost pretty much everything they owned in the fire, this family will always be grateful to the glorious golden for saving their lives. Teddy's motto seems to be, "You scratch my back, I'll scratch yours."

Golden retrievers are one of the most popular dog breeds in the United States.

I'M FELINE FINE!

BINX

WHERE: FRANKLIN, WISCONSIN, U.S.A.

This kitten came into Specialty Purebred Cat Rescue looking more like a fuzzy rodent than a kitten. He was underweight, sick, and super sad. About the size of a small apple, he was not expected to live long. But thanks to the big hearts of his rescuers, this little pip-squeak got a second chance. They gave him oodles of love and care. He was adopted by a devoted family, including a little girl who pushed the kitten around in a stroller, snuggled him, and carried him around the house like a baby. They named him Binx. By the time he was 18 months old, Binx had blossomed from a fuzzy baby into a stunning cat. Binx was actually purebred ragdoll. These cats are known for their floppy, cuddly nature, silky coats, and beautiful blue eyes. He may have started life as an "ugly duckling," but he turned into a beautiful "swan" of a cat.

Ragdoll cats are known for their love of snuggling.

SOCKINGTON
AND PENNYCAT

YOU COULD CALL ME A "CELEBRI-KITTY"!

SOCKINGTON

PENNYCAT

WHERE: **WALTHAM, MASSACHUSETTS, U.S.A.**

These crazy cats tweet more than they meow! Superstar Socks has more than 1.5 million followers on social media. He's made movies, inspired T-shirt art, writes a blog, and loves to dine on sushi. He and his pal Penny use their social-media-star status to help raise money for animals in need and promote animal rescue. Socks's super story starts with a rescue. He was found outside a train station near Boston. The sad little gray and white kitten passed through a few homes before he arrived at his forever home, where he enjoys sunny windowsills, tuna, and trying to win the favor of his housemate, Pennycat. She was adopted by Socks's family after she was left on the front porch of an animal shelter in New York. Look out world—this witty duo has taken the Internet by storm.

DOG KISSES INCOMING!

A dog can earn the American Kennel Club's Canine Good Citizen title by passing a 10-step test for good behavior.

STEVIE
WONDER

WHERE: SALT LAKE CITY, UTAH, U.S.A.

Stevie the wonder dog may be blind, but as a therapy dog he helps people suffering with illness "see" the sunny side of life. He sees the good in everyone, and brings a smile to everyone he meets. But when he was just five weeks old, Stevie's life wasn't so sunny; he had been dropped off at a shelter. Stevie was rescued by the Utah Animal Advocacy Foundation and later adopted by his forever family. His new owners gave him lots of love and training, bringing out the best in him. He loved everybody he met—dogs and humans alike. It wasn't long before Stevie earned his Canine Good Citizen certification from the American Kennel Club. Later he started working as a pet therapy dog, delivering wiggles and wags and kisses and cuddles to people eager to hang with this sensational dog. On his days off, Stevie loves to kiss babies and hike with his family.

BUBBA

WHERE: SAN JOSE, CALIFORNIA, U.S.A.

Amber Marienthal adopted what she thought was a quiet young cat from the San Jose Animal Care Center. Bubba loved his new family, but he was not a happy indoor cat. Nor was he quiet. Bubba would howl, yell, yammer, and meow at the back door until someone let him out. Soon he was exploring—first in his backyard, then his neighbors' yards, and finally at school! These days, Bubba follows his human brother to the neighborhood high school every day. He wears a tracking device so his owner can keep tabs on him. Bubba likes to visit friends in the principal's office, chill in the cafeteria, and lounge on his favorite teachers' desks. He especially loves after-school activities, like watching baseball practice and football games. Last year he was first in line to have his student ID card made. His all-time favorite event? You guessed it—back to school night. Bubba's picture even made it into the school yearbook. One thing's for sure—this tabby's never tardy. He's got *purr*-fect attendance at school.

Feline A.S.B.
Bubba
12
Leland
2015 HIGH SCHOOL 2016

NIBBLES

WHERE: MADERA, CALIFORNIA, U.S.A.

Nibbles the orphaned duck quacks up when his adopted mother—a little boy named Jonny—comes home from school. Every day, the devoted duck waits patiently for classes to finish, then goes to the bus stop to wait for Jonny to get off the school bus. This unlikely pair bonded after Nibbles hatched in Jonny's hand. Sadly, the mother duck had passed away. The chick "imprinted" on Jonny, meaning he thought Jonny was his mother. Even as a grown duck, Nibbles wants to spend every minute with his "mom." But Jonny's not the only thing Nibbles loves. He loves to eat, devouring fresh spring lettuces, watermelon, and grapes. He also slurps worms, crickets, and roaches. He likes fishing, camping, playing in the mud, and swimming with his family, as well as out-ings to the pet store to shop for crickets. And that's not all—he adores getting pedicures. Jonny's mom trims his nails and rubs coconut oil on the duck's webbed feet so they don't dry out. And if he's tired? This lucky duck rides around in a stroller.

Ducks can be found on every continent but Antarctica.

KULI

WHO SAYS CATS HATE THE WATER?

WHERE: **HONOLULU, HAWAII, U.S.A.**

Cat-abunga! This one-eyed cat loves to surf. Rescued from an animal shelter in Hawaii, his adopters named him Nanakuli after a beautiful Hawaiian valley. Nanakuli was very skinny, weighing only about a pound (0.5 kg), and had a badly infected eye. Kuli's first month at home was tough. He gobbled up every bit of food in sight, but threw up so often that he needed baths twice a day to keep his fur clean. Kuli's adopters feared he wouldn't survive. But tough Kuli rallied. Slowly he gained weight. And as for all those baths? His owners believe it taught Kuli to tolerate water. When Kuli began to thrive, they wondered if he might like to go surfing with them. They started by bringing Kuli to a quiet beach with calm water. Then—surf's up. They put a surfboard in the water and let adventurous Kuli sit on it. Standing beside him, Kuli's owners gently splashed water on his paws. Then they taught Kuli to swim. He even had his own life jacket. Now whenever his owners pull out their beach bag, Kuli's in (as in, in the bag!). At the beach, this rad cat lies down on the nose of the board with his paws hanging ten until it's time to catch the next wave.

Surfing is one of the oldest athletic sports in the world.

PAUL

WHERE: **BURHAVE, GERMANY**

This supersweet bovine snuggler couldn't be any happier than when he's cuddling with his favorite human caretakers. That is, unless he's rubbing against the electric back-scratcher for cows, or noshing on a fresh apple. Paul the bull, a permanent resident of an animal sanctuary called Hof Butenland, is a happy camper all around. He arrived as an injured, underfed calf, just two months old. His rescuers convinced his then owner to let him live out a happy life on the farm. Hof Butenland used to be a dairy farm with 60 cows. Now it's a happy retirement home for cows, pigs, horses, ponies, ducks, chickens, geese, rabbits, cats, and dogs. When Paul's not cuddling, hogging the back-scratcher, or chilling and chewing cud with his lady cow friends, this beautiful bull loves to go for walks or just lie in the grass and enjoy the clean country air.

I'M MOOOVIN' IN FOR A HUG.

LADY

WHERE: **ODESSA, FLORIDA, U.S.A.**

This lovely Lady is living large. After finding herself at the Chautauqua County Animal Shelter in Kansas twice, this senior citizen's story came to life online, thanks to social media. When a Florida dog lover read the story, she felt compassion for the old dog, who had endured a tough life. Despite more than 1,300 miles (2,092 km) between the sweet pooch and the Floridian who wanted to give her another chance, the woman sent a private jet to pick Lady up. This good dog got to live out her life in lavish style and with a lot of love and sunshine in Florida.

YOU'RE SAFE WITH ME!

JJ

WHERE: APEX, NORTH CAROLINA, U.S.A.

Originally a shelter dog at the Orange County Animal Shelter, JJ was adopted and trained as an "alert dog" for a little girl who suffers from a cell disorder called mastocytosis. This former pound pup can sense when her young owner is about to have a life-threatening reaction. She alerts everyone to the situation by jumping up and barking. When the girl needed surgery, doctors even let the little fluff ball into the operating room to help them monitor her condition. Everywhere her kid owner goes, JJ follows—to school, to bed, sledding, even to the beach and on an airplane. In return, JJ gets unlimited belly rubs, kisses, and her favorite stuffed squeaky squirrel. What a great deal for them both!

BOB BARKER

WHERE: ARLINGTON, VIRGINIA, U.S.A.

After answering an ad about a Boston terrier–pug puppy for sale, Becky Baines quickly realized something wasn't right. The three-month-old puppy was sniffling, and his eyes were red. He was filthy and stinky and had been living in a bathtub his entire life. Even so, it was love at first sight. Becky was able to convince the backyard breeder (so-called because these people often breed dogs illegally within their own homes) to relinquish the puppy to her. The puppy, now named Bob Barker, was in worse shape than Becky had thought. He had ear mites, worms, and an infection. But with love, patience, vet care, and a bath, Becky nursed the tiny terrier to health. Bob went from a scared, shy puppy to a happy pooch. These days, Bob is not only healthy, but a model to boot! Becky decided to show off Bob's unique looks by dressing him in costumes and taking photos. For the holidays, she gives out calendars that feature the handsome hound. And once, Bob even modeled for the cover of *National Geographic Kids* magazine! When he's not being featured on magazines, Bob serves as a role model for adoptable dogs everywhere, proving that needy pets can be the best pets.

Bob was once photographed by a famous National Geographic photographer.

BELLA

WHERE: WASHINGTON, D.C., U.S.A.

In the nation's capital, Homeward Trails Animal Rescue kitty #4994 started out alone and unprotected. But thanks to the rescue group that cared for her, she now spends her days surrounded with love and attention. The young cat waited for weeks in an adoption display area at a pet-supply store. Super friendly, this kitty who loves to flop, snuggle, and head-butt hoped that one of the friendly faces looking in might give her a home. That December, the hopeful kitty got a holiday wish: A kind man brought her home to his family and gave her a forever home. Named Bella, this comfy kitty now lives a posh, pampered life. She gets daily massages, sleeps on soft blankets, and watches birds from her favorite sunny windowsill. She also has her own security detail, sort of like how Secret Service agents guard the president at the White House not far away. At Bella's house, two big German shepherds protect, watch, listen, and follow. They keep their adoring eyes on her every move.

A recent study ranked German shepherds as the third most intelligent dog breed.

SUPER SPORTIES

Thanks to hardworking and dedicated animal rescuers, pets who've had a tough start still have a chance for a good life. Take these super sports stars, for example. Each one had their own challenges. But watch out—they've all made a big comeback—on the sports field and off!

WHAT A WEIRD GAME OF FETCH.

SUPER TEDDY AND OSCAR

WHERE: AUCKLAND, NEW ZEALAND

These former rescue pups got to be ball boys at a tennis tournament. They worked like dogs—racing to fetch balls, carrying tennis rackets, and delivering water bottles for tennis pro Venus Williams.

The cute pups got the job after organizers asked their owner, animal trainer Mark Vette, to provide trained canines for a television commercial being filmed at the event. He brought Oscar, a goofy but obedient bull mastiff cross, and a comical rescued terrier mix named Super Teddy.

After weeks of training, the stars were ready for their gig. Mark taught them to run into the game only when the ball hit the net on their side of the court. They may have slobbered too much, but they did a grand slam job. Especially when Teddy lobbed Venus a big kiss across the face. In tennis, that's what you call a score of "love–love."

ZODIAC

WHERE: GAITHERSBURG, MARYLAND, U.S.A.

A winning racehorse originally named Rhythmic Moves, Zodiac earned more than $200,000 during his racing career but was retired after an injury to his right front leg. But the animals at his retirement home weren't well cared for. They went hungry and suffered serious neglect. Animal control officers impounded the horses. They were in terrible shape. Lucky Zodiac ended up at Days End Farm Horse Rescue. With a lot of TLC and vet care, the horse slowly recovered. A volunteer named Jean took a special interest in Zodiac. She fed him, groomed him, and walked him around the farm when she visited every weekend. Little by little, the miracle horse recovered. Jean adopted him and gave him a forever home. Now Zodiac lives in a beautiful pasture with other horse pals. He loves to race around the field and provides his loving owner with what she says is "unlimited happiness."

An organization called Canter helps retired racehorses in the United States find new jobs.

Greyhounds can run up to 45 miles an hour (72 km/h), but they would often rather nap than race.

CINDY

WHERE: MIAMI, FLORIDA, U.S.A.

When a homeless puppy born on a racetrack needed a rescue, Hollydogs Greyhound Adoption stepped in. The group found her a wonderful adoptive home when she was six months old. This sporty girl—Soaring Cindy—found her calling competing in agility and high jumping. She could clear a barrier nearly six feet (1.8 m) tall—more than twice her height. Thanks to her drive (and her strong legs), the high-flying pooch is a record holder for high-jumping dogs. Cindy also competed in flying disc, was a spokesdog for rescue and animal adoption, was a therapy dog, and even appeared in a commercial. Way to bring your A-game, Cindy! This good girl passed away not too long ago, after living a long and healthy life. She was loved by everyone who met her.

SAMSON

WHERE: LONG ISLAND, NEW YORK, U.S.A.

At four months old, a Czech shepherd was bumped from an explosives detection dog training program because of a minor heart murmur. Dogs in the program train hard and work hard. Samson's medical problem got in the way. Samson ended up at the Washington Animal Rescue League in Washington, D.C., with the hope that he would end up as a pet instead of a working dog. And Samson wasn't homeless for long; when former New York City Police officer John Del Pozzo heard about the wonderful dog, he and his family made tracks. Mom, Dad, three kids, and their dog Amber all drove five hours to meet Samson. It was meant to be—Amber and the kids got a new sibling, and Dad got a retirement buddy. Several hours later, the family (including Samson) hit the road back toward home. Today, attentive, obedient Samson loves "retirement," especially when it involves his tennis balls, his doggie neighbors, and all his new siblings.

MOE

WHERE: WASHINGTON, D.C., U.S.A.

When Lilly Chapa saw a beautiful bearded dragon listed as available for adoption at the Washington Humane Society, she reached out to his foster parent to get more details. Because of poor care from his previous owner, the lizard had a condition that gave him a hunchback appearance. He might have to be euthanized. That's when Lilly knew she had to adopt this cold-blooded cutie. These days, Moe's hunched back never gets in his way. In fact, his life couldn't be better. He loves eating crickets, worms, and vegetables, and sunning himself on his favorite rock. He also likes sprinting around his home and sleeping under the radiator in the winter. When the weather is nice, Moe sits on his owner's shoulder for a walk to the park. He also loves to attack shoelaces or other wiggly objects that look like fun. Go Moe!

MEALWORMS, ANYONE?

A bearded dragon's "beard" is not really a beard—it's dark, spiny skin that puffs out if the lizard feels threatened.

PWDDITAT

WHERE: ANGLESEY, NORTH WALES, U.K.

One day, a stray kitty showed up on the doorstep of an elderly cat owner. She welcomed him in. The cat, whom she named Pwdditat (pronounced Puddi-tat), made a beeline for the woman's blind chocolate Labrador mix. The dog, named Terfel, had suffered abuse during his life before finding shelter at the woman's home. Now he was an old dog who rarely left his bed. But Pwdditat seemed to have other plans for good old Terf. Pwdditat became his best friend, and was always affectionate with the gentle-natured dog. Soon the sweet cat had appointed himself Terfel's guide cat. All on his own, Pwdditat began coaxing the fearful dog out of his bed and leading him around the yard. Every so often, Pwdditat would stop and nudge Terfel forward or wind around his legs to reassure him. Terfel had trust in his feline friend. They took short excursions together, the elderly dog relying on his cat to guide him. The pair continues to live long into old age alongside each other, cuddling, nuzzling, and taking each other for walks.

Puppy love is a real thing—when you look a puppy in the eyes, its brain releases a "love hormone."

THOR

WHERE: SOUTHPORT, NORTH CAROLINA, U.S.A.

That Saturday when his owners packed up to go out of town, Thor had other plans. Thor, whose family had adopted him from Southport–Oak Island Animal Rescue, had gone out for a walk but was reluctant to come back inside, which was unusual for the very obedient dog. He went inside, but then pounded on the door demanding to go back out. Confused by his behavior, his owners, now late to leave on their trip, let him outside again. The dog ran out of the house, stopped to look back at his owners, then barked, as if to say, "This way!" He then ran around the corner. His owners followed. When they caught up, they found the dog tending to an elderly neighbor who had fallen on the way to her mailbox. She was in bad shape. They called 911. They also credited their gentle, smart, quick-thinking dog for saving the lady's life. She said she had been yelling for help, but Thor was the only "person" who came to the rescue. Thor's owners can't say enough good things about their treasured pet—he's a true superhero.

LUNA

WHERE: McKINNEY, TEXAS, U.S.A.

A Chihuahua pup named Luna survived a scary ordeal when someone left her by the side of the road sealed in a cardboard box. Lucky for the pup, a curious driver stopped and picked up the box. When he opened it, a frightened little dog with big brown eyes peered out. The trembling puppy ended up at the Collin County Animal Shelter. Fortunately, a big-hearted shelter volunteer offered to foster the scared girl immediately. Even though she refused to come out of her crate and was terrified of most people, Luna's foster family showed her nothing but love and care (and lots of treats). Soon Luna gave them a chance. Now she has the life she always deserved. She's a pampered daddy's girl, adopted by her foster parents and their houseful of pets. She has toys, pretty outfits, and even a "pee-pee tent" outside so she won't get rained on when she has to do her business in bad weather! Her favorite place to hang out? Stretching out in the lap of luxury—as in, on a fluffy blanket in her dad's lap.

Chihuahuas are descendants of a breed of dog that lived in Mexico in the ninth century.

JUST CALL ME QUEEN OF THE JUNGLE.

NALA

WHERE: LOS ANGELES, CALIFORNIA, U.S.A.

This social media star has nearly three million followers, but she actually started out as a sick, abandoned rescue kitty taken in by a shelter. Thanks to her owner, who loves to snap her pic, Nala is showing the world how good life can be for a once sad and hungry kitten. She doesn't have to fend for herself anymore. Nope, her days are filled with lounging; eating sushi; modeling snazzy bandannas, bow ties, and hats; and doing important work inside paper bags. But it's not all fun and paper bags for Nala. She's also helping her owner fund-raise and spread the word about the importance of animal rescue. And during her time off from modeling and fund-raising, she loves to play fetch, just like a dog. No matter what she's doing, this little princess is *feline* fine.

I ACCEPT KIBBLE AS MY BABYSITTING WAGES.

BOOTS

WHERE: PHOENIX, ARIZONA, U.S.A.

This chow–golden retriever mix was found homeless after a terrible hurricane and taken to a local shelter. A volunteer at the shelter adopted him and put him to work as a volunteer, too. Now kittens climb all over Boots the rescue dog like he's a furry, 45-pound (20.4-kg) jungle gym. A sort of nanny, Boots interacts with the shelter cats at the Arizona Humane Society to prepare them for being around other animals when they're adopted.

The kittens chase his tail, climb on his back, play with his collar, and knead their little paws on his belly. For these homeless kittens, Boots is a regular kitty-sitter. But no matter what you call him, one thing's for sure: This sweet pooch is the cat's meow.

Young kittens sleep up to 16 hours a day.

HANDSOME DAN

WHERE: PROVIDENCE, RHODE ISLAND, U.S.A.

When 22 dogs arrived at Best Friends Animal Society from an illegal dog-fighting ring, they needed time to recover from the cruel treatment they'd endured. One of these dogs, Dan the sweet young pit bull, feared people but not other dogs. Because Dan lacked confidence, a trainer decided to call him "Handsome Dan" to remind everyone (and Dan!) of his amazing potential. When he was adopted, his new family knew they'd need to be patient for this sweet boy to trust humans again. But Dan settled in. He relaxed and played with his canine siblings and adjusted to life with people little by little. In his new home, he seemed to realize he was free to be puppy-ish and playful. Handsome Dan's transformation inspired his family to rescue more dogs. They started an organization in his name, called Handsome Dan's Rescue. The organization provides help with care, training, and finding homes for dogs in local shelters. Way to go, Dan!

WOOF! ... I MEAN, MEOW!

SOPHIE AND SIDNEY

WHERE: MEDFIELD, MASSACHUSETTS, U.S.A.

Sophie the rescue dog hadn't been in her new home for long when her adoptive family brought her the best present ever: a very small but sweet and cuddly kitten. Sophie's new family didn't know much about the dog's life before adoption, just that the chow-spitz mix had probably been abused and that she had had a litter of puppies. Supersweet and very maternal Sophie *loved* having a kitten to care for. She carried baby Sidney around by the scruff of his neck, snuggled with him, and gently guided his every move. The kitten—who started out small but grew up to look like a little bear cub—grew up thinking he was a dog. He loved to sleep on Sophie's bed, go for walks outdoors, and instead of purring, that canine-ish cat would wag his tail.

TOBY

WHERE: CENTRE HALL, PENNSYLVANIA, U.S.A.

The night this sad, homeless pony found his forever home, he was for sale at an auction in a cramped pen. When a lady named Annette Traband walked by, the pony knocked down a bucket, kicked it over, and stepped up on it to get her attention. It was like he was saying, "Pick me! Pick me!" Annette seemed to hear the pony. She brought him home the next day and named him Toby. Over the next few years, her daughter, Lizzy, trained Toby to do tricks like riding without a bridle, bowing, and hugging her. The determined pair worked hard and eventually joined up with a trick rider for performances around the United States. Now that his girl is getting ready to go to college, this star sport-pony has retired from competitions and performances and lives a life of leisure. He only has to work once in a while for fun, like pulling a sleigh when it snows. He has tons of care and spends his days with his friend Puddles (another pony) in a field outside of Lizzy's bedroom window.

Horses have been domesticated for more than 5,000 years.

BEST FRIENDS
ANIMAL SOCIETY

With so many needy animals around the globe, it takes a lot of time, dedication, and love to make a difference. That's where Best Friends Animal Society comes in. Started in the 1980s, Best Friends currently runs the largest no-kill sanctuary for pets in the United States, and aims to make it so that pets are no longer killed in shelters. Read on to find out about some of the many amazing animals they have saved!

JUSTIN

WHERE: KANAB, UTAH, U.S.A.

Justin is just like any other nibbly puppy, except for one—well, two—things: He was born without his two rear paws. Found underneath a house as a tiny pup, Justin (now called Jax) was bottle fed by a kind person and brought to Best Friends. There, the staff dedicated their time to helping Justin grow strong and healthy. Justin began physical therapy, including his favorite activity of swimming, which helped strengthen the muscles and bones in his back legs. Justin also enjoyed playing with other dogs, practicing walking on thick blankets, and nibbling on staff fingertips. Soon, nothing was stopping Justin—he was even able to walk around by balancing on his front paws. And not long after that, this two-pawed pup walked right into the heart of a woman from California, and found himself a new name and a new home. For now, Justin gets around with the help of a pair of bright red booties. Soon he will be fitted for a wheelchair, and once he is completely grown, he'll get brand-new prosthetic legs. Nothing can stop this pup!

Some dogs have harmless bacteria on their feet that make them smell like corn chips!

KING O.

WHERE: KANAB, UTAH, U.S.A.

King O. is a ducorps cockatoo with a big voice and even bigger personality. King O. (O for Ophelia) had a loving home with a doting elderly woman, but sadly fell on hard times when his person passed away. King O.'s new people were unable to give the beautiful bird the attention, affection, and care that he needed. The poor cockatoo became so distressed that he began to pluck out his own feathers and scream loudly for attention. But luckily for King O., he was soon able to put his voice to good use. After being rescued by Best Friends, King O. discovered a new love: singing. As he grew happier and healthier at the sanctuary, King O. took to singing along with his favorite jams. Soon he was even dancing. The bopping bird loves to bob his head and replace the words to songs with his own name. And better yet, this cockatoo king now has a permanent, loving home where he can croon all day. King O. is a smash hit!

Some types of birds perform coordinated dances with their mates.

I'M THE PRESIDENT OF THE UNITED STATES OF CUTENESS!

ROOSEVELT

WHERE: KANAB, UTAH, U.S.A.

When a pregnant stray cat was brought to Best Friends, she gave birth to a tiny kitten with a big name. Sadly, the mama cat had arrived in labor with a broken pelvis, so she and most of the litter didn't make it, but the Best Friends caregivers named the surviving kitten Roosevelt. Roosevelt required constant care: He needed food every two hours, and was so small that he had to be fed with a medical syringe. But little Roosevelt had a big spirit, and he survived. Each day, Roosevelt grew a bit stronger, thanks to his caregivers' attention. They groomed the tiny kitten's fur with a toothbrush, and gave him teddy bears as companions. His caretakers even gave him a cake to celebrate his one-month birthday. Soon, Roosevelt's fighting spirit earned him a permanent home with a caretaker's mom. Under the adoring eyes of his new family, Roosevelt grew from a tiny kitten to a handsome cat that fit his large name. But don't worry—the now-big kitten is still as spoiled as ever; his new life still includes teddy bears, cuddles, and cakes for his birthdays.

I PLEDGE ALLEGIANCE TO THE RED, WHITE, AND CHEW!

CARLOS

WHERE: COLORADO SPRINGS, COLORADO, U.S.A.

Sweet Carlos was the last dog left in a kennel in Afghanistan. He had spent most of his life working as an explosives detection dog. During his five years of military service, the dog had worked hard to save human lives by searching vehicles, buildings, and other dangerous areas to find hidden explosive devices in the Middle East. By the time he was eight years old, he was ready to retire from work, but had no home. Around the same time, Ruby Ridpath and her husband, a retired military man, saw a program on television about people adopting retired military dogs. They wanted to adopt one, too. The first time Carlos met his new family was at the airport, and it was love at first sight. The sweet dog got right down to enjoying his retirement, from playing fetch to taking long naps. Carlos still liked to work, too. He visited schools and made special appearances as a war dog ambassador. He even traveled to Washington, D.C., to represent dogs of war in front of Congress. Heroic Carlos lived out the rest of his life in his happy home, bringing smiles to everyone he met.

DILL AND PICKLES

WHERE: LOS ANGELES, CALIFORNIA, U.S.A.

Two little dogs living on their own in a trash heap helped each other survive by sticking together. When rescuers from Hope for Paws approached the pair of pups, they seemed relieved to be found. The pups had every right to be scared and wary, but as long as they were together, they accepted food and attention. Rescuers named the male Dill and put a leash over his head. They named the female Pickles. She was happy to have a leash on if her friend did, too. And to coax Pickles into a waiting car, rescuers carried Dill in front of her—she kept walking and wagging her tail as long as Dill was in sight! Dill and Pickles got adopted into different homes, but don't fret—they live in the same neighborhood. The devoted pair, no longer lonesome or hungry, can now focus on the important things in life, like playdates, picnics, and long walks.

PICKLES

DILL

REY

WHERE: SALT LAKE CITY, UTAH, U.S.A.

This smiley-faced kitten is sunshine all the time! Rescued as a teeny tiny stray kitten by Best Friends Animal Society, she was nursed back to health with her brother and sister before she was available for adoption. It didn't take long before this little ray of sunshine found a forever home. She immediately brightened the mood of her grateful adoptive family, which included two adult cats. Her new owners loved her furry, friendly face. The little star, named Rey, after the Star Wars character, settled right in at home. Wanting to spread her sunshine to the world, Rey's adopted parents started snapping pictures of her lounging, playing, snuggling, chasing her squeaky mouse, and of course—smiling. Now she has thousands of fans who follow her ray of light on social media. As for Rey, with her permanently upturned mouth and fantastic forever home—she can't stop smiling!

Cats can relieve stress, calm nerves, and lower blood pressure in humans.

MANNY

WHERE: NEW YORK, NEW YORK, U.S.A.

In the summer of 2015, a starving homeless black cat found himself in terrible trouble. He was stuck more than 30 stories above the East River, on New York City's Manhattan Bridge. An office worker in a nearby office building spotted the cat and called the Animal Care Centers of NYC. The rescue group asked the city's Department of Transportation (DOT) for help. DOT staff closed a lane of traffic on the bridge then baited a trap with cat food. But the hungry kitty was too scared to move. One worker crawled up and lured him into the trap. At the emergency vet clinic, a vet examined the poor cat. He had an eye injury and wounds old and new. With help from the Mayor's Alliance for NYC's Animals, the cat (named Manny) got the help he needed. Now he's healthy again, even if he is missing an eye. His rescuers gave him a chance for a great future. Thanks to them, this super kitty's *feline* fine again.

CHRIS P. BACON

WHERE: SUMTERVILLE, FLORIDA, U.S.A.

Chris P. Bacon the potbellied pig is always ready to roll—literally. Born with hind legs that don't quite work, Chris has a set of wheels that can be attached to his back end to help him get around.

The orphaned piglet got his ride after being adopted by a veterinarian. Walking was very hard for the little oinker, so his new owner used pieces from a toy building set to make Chris a tiny pig-mobile: a brace made of short plastic rods that connected to a small seat between two wheels. Gently strapped in, soon Chris could cruise. His owner later found a company to make a sturdier metal setup for Chris. Now he spends his time taking walks and chasing toads. When he wants a rest, the wheels come off—this piggy likes napping as much as roaming.

Pigs use their snouts to root for food and explore the world around them.

SAMMIE

WHERE: DALLAS, TEXAS, U.S.A.

When Sammie ran away from his original owners, he seemed to know he was heading toward a better life. His then owners didn't give poor Sammie enough care or attention, and left Sammie outside alone in the stifling Texas heat. So the plucky Pomeranian dug himself an escape tunnel and struck out toward freedom. Soon after, he arrived at the home of a Good Samaritan whose nieces, Allie and Penny Nambo, happened to love dogs. The family located Sammie's original owners, only to be told that his then owners no longer even wanted the little guy. Luckily, Allie and Penny were ready to step in! Now Sammie's life is better than even he could have dreamed when he first made his daring escape more than 10 years ago. Sammie—now 14 years old—still loves to explore, too. He goes hiking (often in his favorite dinosaur costume), enjoys sledding in stylish winter gear, and sometimes likes to walk on his two hind legs to get a better view of the world around him. And when he's excited (which is often), Sammie spins in circles. But as much as he loves to explore, this courageous cutie's favorite thing to do is come home to snuggle.

LEO, CRUMPET, AND MOCHA

CRUMPET

LEO

MOCHA

Happy bunnies like to "binky": they will run, jump, and quickly turn 180 degrees in midair.

WHERE: WARRENTON, VIRGINIA, U.S.A.

This unlikely rabbit family went from barely surviving to being super spoiled. Crumpet, a lovable mixed breed, had been dropped off at City Wildlife, a wildlife rehabilitation center. Crumpet was in bad shape. Slowly, he regained his health and got a little more used to having people care for him. He was soon adopted by a bunny-loving family. Meanwhile, Leo grew up hidden away in a college dorm room until he was discovered, and his owner was told to find him a new home. One thing led to another and the friendly brown Holland lop was rescued by the same family in Virginia. Their owners adored the pair from the start, but were in for a huge surprise. One day, they discovered a nest of baby bunnies in their rabbits' hutch—it turns out that Leo was a girl, and she was now a mama bunny! Luckily, the family was able to keep many of the baby bunnies, and they adopted the rest out to loving homes. These days, Leo and Crumpet scamper around the goat yard and lounge side by side in the deluxe rabbit hutch that they share. Their babies are equally spoiled—especially Mocha Ray Tyler, a fuzzy-headed cutie with a gorgeous mane. This brave bunny loves going for walks outside like a dog—she even has her own custom red harness and leash! When she's not strutting her stuff, Mocha enjoys sharing sweet strawberries and fresh salads with her doting owner. These rascally rabbits are living the good life!

CALLIE

WHERE: ROCHESTER, WASHINGTON, U.S.A.

When a tiny lamb was too small and sickly to be sold, a Good Samaritan brought her to Puget Sound Goat Rescue. Callie arrived with the joints in her front legs so infected that she couldn't walk. The vet said she might be disabled forever. Caregivers at the rescue treated her sickness, kept her comfortable, and built a cart for Callie so she could get around. She took to the cart like a champ, taking the weight off of her painful front legs. Over the months, a miraculous transformation took place. The little lamb began to walk on her own again. She was adopted into a wonderful home, along with other lucky goats and sheep from the same rescue. These days, Callie spends her days frolicking and snacking with friends. She shares a pasture with a rescued donkey. What does Callie think of this cushy new life? Not *baaa*d!

AFTER

China has the most sheep of any country.

BEFORE

MAGILL

WHERE: WASHINGTON, D.C., U.S.A.

When staff at the Washington Animal Rescue League noticed a homeless white cat in the alley, they worried she might be hungry. They also worried about the weather. A "polar vortex" was causing bone-chilling temperatures that January, which almost certainly spelled disaster for a little kitty left outdoors. Staff tried to catch her, but the kitty ran away when anyone tried to approach. They then tried setting up a humane trap in the snow, but the smart cat managed to get the food without getting caught. Finally, one very cold day, a staff member tried to lure the cat in with just food in a cat carrier. It worked! They rushed her into the clinic and got her vetted, and named her Magill. She turned out to be super friendly and not scared of humans at all. It wasn't long before an adopter fell in love with the spunky girl. She settled in quickly to her new home, slept on her new owner's bed from the very first night, and now loves to chase her toy mouse and attack her owner's knitting projects. And as for snow, from now on, this pretty kitty is content to watch it from her favorite windowsill.

SUNNY

WHERE: CROPSEY, ILLINOIS, U.S.A.

Nobody knows how the abandoned filly ended up on the side of the road early that September morning. Kelsey Allonge and her mother were driving along at 5:30 a.m. when something told them to take a different route. When they spotted a thin and injured young horse grazing on the side of the road, the Allonges stopped to see what was up. After deciding that the horse was in bad shape and in need of a rescue, Kelsey walked the waifish youngster nine miles (14.5 km) back to their farm. It took four hours, but the needy horse seemed to know she was walking to a better place. They named her Sunny because the horse had a bright future. Kelsey slept in the barn with Sunny for the first five nights. Fortunately, her road to recovery was smooth. Sunny ate and gained weight, and her cuts and scrapes healed. Now fully recovered, Sunny has grown up to be a sweet and beautiful pet. She has learned to carry a rider and jump over obstacles. She competes in horse shows and is inspiring lots of smiles. This happy horse's name in the show ring? My Little Sunshine.

HISTORIC HOUNDS

There's an endless list of ways that dogs help people, such as helping them see, comforting them, and even protecting them in times of war. Check out these heroic rescue hounds whose histories have passed the test of time.

SERGEANT STUBBY

This heroic war dog lived almost 100 years ago and served in France during World War I. He was the mutt-tastic mascot of the 102nd Infantry, named for his stubby tail. He'd been smuggled into the army by his owner, Private Robert Conroy, who had rescued the stray terrier mix back in the United States. One day in the fall of 1918, Stubby, who had been accepted by the army camp as a mascot, was napping near a trench. He woke up quickly when a German spy snuck in. Stubby leapt up and bit the man's rear end, then hung on until help arrived. That night, the dog was given high honors and the title of Sergeant. Stubby took his job very seriously. He even learned to salute by raising his paw.

Sergeant Stubby was the first dog to be given rank in the U.S. armed forces.

SMOKY

This little World War II heroine had a giant heart. She was originally found by a soldier, scared and tiny in a war-torn jungle on a Pacific Island. Another soldier won the four-pound (1.8-kg) dog in a card game. He named the dog Smoky, carried her in his backpack, and shared his food rations with the teeny pup. He also taught her hilarious tricks that entertained the soldiers and kept their spirits up. Once when her owner and other soldiers puzzled over how to string a critical telephone wire through a pipe under an airstrip, Smoky came to the rescue. When her owner gave her the command, she carried the wire into one side of the narrow pipe and 70 feet (21.3 m) out the other. It was a dangerous mission, but it saved 250 soldiers from putting themselves at risk to dig out the pipe. This small but mighty war dog survived 18 months of combat, then came home to the United States with her owner where she lived out her days as a pampered pint-size princess.

Smoky's famous tricks included walking on a tightrope blindfolded, spelling her name, riding a scooter, playing dead, and singing on command!

JUDY

Born in Shanghai, China, this English pointer became a friendly mascot for a British Royal Navy ship based there. But Judy's life was not to be all snuggles and cuddles. In 1942, the ship she was on was bombed by Japanese planes and the passengers had to abandon ship. Survivors, including Judy who had helped soldiers swim to safety, were marooned on an island in the South China Sea for two days without food or water. Judy saved them from dying of thirst by sniffing out and digging up a freshwater spring. The group ended up on a boat to Sumatra, where they were captured. The humans in the prison with Judy hid her behind sacks of rice. A prisoner named Frank Williams shared his food with the dog. She never left his side. The prisoners took heart from their special companion. She helped protect them, too, from the guards and wild animals around the camp. When they were finally rescued in 1944, Frank had to smuggle Judy onboard the ship home. Back in the U.K., heroic Judy was met with fanfare and great fame. The great war dog lived with Frank for the rest of her life.

In 1946 the British government awarded Judy the Dickin Medal, which honors the extraordinary wartime service of animals.

AFTER

DOMINIC

WHERE: HUME, VIRGINIA, U.S.A.

When the Middleburg Humane Foundation took in a pregnant donkey named Katie, it wasn't long before they had a baby donkey on their hands. But he came with a big surprise—a serious birth defect that would require surgery to save his life. Rescue workers fretted and stressed about his recovery. Volunteers babysat him overnight and raised money to pay for his veterinary care. After surgery, he stayed close to his mother and nursed like a champ. Soon he began to thrive and play, buck, run, and get into mischief. A wonderful family with a farm applied to adopt baby Dominic and his mother. His new family thinks everything the dapper donkey does is super cute. Like how he curls up with his adopted brother, another baby donkey named Lester, to sleep. And how he loves to admire himself in a mirror in the barn. Nobody disagrees with Dominic that he is super-duper donkey-kicking cute.

BEFORE

SAM

WHERE: NEW YORK, NEW YORK, U.S.A.

This cat might look worried, but he doesn't have a care in the world. He's living the high life as a supermodel cat. Rescued off the streets of New York City, Sam found a new home fast after winding up in a shelter. After being adopted, the cat quickly made himself comfortable in his new home. He melted in his adopter's arms and she gave him a new life. When a friend commented on his big black "eyebrows" and his expressive face, Sam's new owner started snapping pics and posting them online. His distinctive black markings make great face. Now he's got thousands of followers who love to "like" his photos on social media! But don't think all the fame has gone to his head. These days Sam keeps it real by running around his cushy home and lounging in a pet stroller while his owners garden. His favorite food? He's bonkers for juicy fresh tomatoes.

TOFFEE AND TRUFFLES

WHERE: NEWARK, DELAWARE, U.S.A.

When a police officer found a sad, skinny, and scruffy puppy tied to a tree, he took her straight to the First State Animal Center and SPCA. Caregivers took in the green-eyed gal and gave her lots of TLC. Soon she was adopted by a veterinarian and his family. They brought the new pup home, named her Toffee, and covered her with kisses. Toffee's new pad was pretty posh—complete with kids to play with, a big basket of toys, dog beds on every floor, and a great yard for romping. A few months after Toffee moved in, a friend of the family heard about a skinny, flea-ridden look-alike pup at another local shelter, the Brandywine Valley SPCA. This second scruffy girl had been found running alongside a road. Didn't Toffee need a sister? Of course she did! The family adopted her, too. Now Truffles loves wrestling with Toffee, giving kisses to everyone she meets, and cuddling under the covers in her human's bed. Toffee and Truffles may not be blood relatives, but they're super snuggle-bunny sisters at heart.

TOFFEE

TRUFFLES

TAFFY, MOO, OLI, AND BOWIE

OLI   EDDY   MOO

BOWIE

TAFFY

WHERE: VANCOUVER, BRITISH COLUMBIA, CANADA

This bunny bunch is living the dream! When a young couple adopted two bunnies named Rambo and Eddy, they came to love them like family. When Rambo and Eddy passed away, their human parents wanted to honor the bunnies' legacies. They continued to adopt bunnies who needed homes, and they now have four bundles of fluff: Moo, who was abandoned at a park but these days is treated like a princess; Oli, who came from an unwanted litter and now loves to sleep on windowsills; Taffy, who was saved as an infant but has grown into a bouncing ball of energy; and Bowie, who recovered from extreme neglect to become a cuddly bunny that loves sleeping in fresh laundry. Together, this fluffy foursome is taking the social media world by storm! Devoted fans get to see pictures of the furry family wearing bunny-size hats, playing with Slinkys, and cuddling with stuffed animals. The bunnies also raise awareness about animal adoption and proper rabbit care. Good work, bunnies—Rambo and Eddy would be proud!

KAI

WHERE: **SAN ANTONIO, TEXAS, U.S.A.**

A playful black Labrador retriever named Kai found herself surrendered to the Humane Society of Central Illinois when her owner couldn't handle the pup's energetic nature. A staff member wondered if busy Kai needed a job to harness her strengths. It was a lucky break for the sweet, homeless dog. She ended up in an arson dog program. The program trains dogs to sniff out substances used to start fires. After 200 hours of training, Kai became a partner to an investigator with the San Antonio Fire Department. Now Kai is a star, especially during an emergency. She maintains her focus despite chaotic scenes involving extreme heat, smoke, bright lights, and loud noise. On the scene, her job is to seek out evidence—like a melted gasoline container—to show how a fire might have started. When Kai's not busy showing the world how much a dog can accomplish when given training and exercise, this hardworking gal takes it easy with her family at home.

In 2014, the American Humane Association Hero Dog Awards named Kai the Arson Dog of the Year.

LITTLE KRATOS

WHERE: **SEAFORD, DELAWARE, U.S.A.**

When a tiny kitten got separated from his mom and had a scary tangle with a forklift at a construction site, a Good Samaritan rushed him to the Veterinary Specialty Center of Delaware. The mother cat had given birth under a storage container that was lifted up and relocated. After the disastrous move, the unlucky kitten, later named Little Kratos, had a badly broken leg. A vet worked magic with a quick cast and pain medication, but eventually the leg had to be amputated. When his rescuer returned to check on Little Kratos, he couldn't help but adopt the kitten. Little Kratos is thriving in his home. He loves to chase pen lights and his dog siblings' tails, and loves hanging like a monkey from his cat tree—all with only three legs!

TOTALLY RAD, DUDE.

DIDGA

WHERE: NEW SOUTH WALES, AUSTRALIA

When Hollywood animal trainer Robert Dollwet adopted a 13-week-old kitten from a shelter, he was looking for a cat he could train for "acting" roles. He found the perfect star-to-be in Didga (short for "didgeridoo," an Australian musical instrument). She was confident, energetic, and smart. To train her, he held out meaty tidbits to encourage her to step forward, jump up, step back, and other tricks. Before long, Didga was jumping up into his hands and walking on a leash. Then Miss Smarty taught herself to skateboard. One day she jumped on a board and rolled around the house. When her owner stopped laughing, he got an idea. Could he combine cat training, gravity, and trick photography to make a series of funny videos? Set to music, they appear to show Didga zipping up and down ramps, shredding half pipes, and jumping obstacles at a skateboard park. One video even shows the furry athlete doing a "hippy jump" over the back of a friendly Rottweiler. How's that for star quality?

In 2015 Didga set a Guinness World Record for performing the most tricks by a cat in one minute, like high-five, shake, roll over, and spin.

DOBBY

The Maltese is one of the oldest known dog breeds.

WHERE: NEW CASTLE, DELAWARE, U.S.A.

When Delaware's Animal Care and Control brought a little Maltese mix to a vet for emergency care, he was in such bad shape that no one dared hope he would live. He had been picked up on the side of the highway. He was malnourished and suffering from bad injuries. But this dogged little survivor still managed to wag his tail. For four days, the staff at Veterinary Specialty Center of Delaware dedicated themselves to their tiny patient in critical care. He was named Dobby, after the character in the Harry Potter book series, for his unwavering love despite his rough start in life. When Dobby was healthy enough to leave, one staff member couldn't resist fostering him. This tiny super-snuggler quickly became part of the pack and a permanent resident. Now Dobby is a pampered pet. He loves chewing the noses off his stuffed animals and snacking. He even goes to work with his owner sometimes and helps to comfort other sick dogs at the same vet clinic that saved him.

NORA

WHERE: PHILADELPHIA, PENNSYLVANIA, U.S.A.

This darling diva started piano lessons early, tapping the piano keys as a freshly adopted kitten. She plays whenever the mood strikes her, even if her adoptive mother is teaching a student to play. About a year after her adoption into the family, her humans caught her playing something like "Twinkle, Twinkle, Little Star," providing accompaniment and entertainment for her owner's students. This budding Beethoven has gone viral on the Internet. But when she's not tickling the ivories, she's busy being a regular (and sometimes grouchy) cat who loves her toys and goes crazy for catnip.

REPTILE RESCUE CENTER

AESOP

WHERE: LITTLE ROCK, ARKANSAS, U.S.A.

The world of pet rescue wouldn't be complete without rockin' reptiles. Because these cold-blooded cuties require special attention, many reptiles sadly are not properly cared for. Luckily, the dedicated people who work at the Reptile Rescue Center devote their efforts to caring for previously unwanted reptiles. The rescue's private facility in Little Rock, Arkansas, is home to more than 100 reptiles of 30 different species. This reptile-rescuing sanctuary takes in homeless and stray reptiles, nurses them back to health, and then rehomes them either with new owners or in the rescue's permanent sanctuary. Lucky lizards (and snakes, tortoises, and turtles) who call the sanctuary home include Beatrice the green iguana, Sunshine the albino Burmese python, Aesop the Greek tortoise, and many more! The Reptile Rescue Center also works to educate the public on reptiles, their proper care, and conservation. Rock on!

BEATRICE

A snake has up to 400 vertebrae along its back; a human has 26.

SUNSHINE

OVERCOMING ODDS

Life can be hard for an animal with a disability. He or she might need more care than the average pet, expensive medicine, or special training. Check out these awesome stories of pets who've weathered serious challenges. With a lot of heart and a lot of help, they persevered, putting one paw in front of the other to make it through from sadness to sunshine.

> When he's not working, Charlie loves to swim at the beach.

CHARLIE

WHERE: SANTA MONICA, CALIFORNIA, U.S.A.

This deaf dalmatian bounced from several homes before landing at a shelter in New York. The people who surrendered him said he was uncontrollable and gave up on him. Dogs with disabilities sometimes need special care and different ways to communicate. When a heroic human named Colleen Wilson heard about this spotty dog's plight, she gave him his hope back. She also gave him the skills he needed to be the perfect pet. Colleen started by teaching him sign language so they could communicate. Now Charlie knows more than 30 sign language commands, including heel, sit, and speak. When his owner gives the sign for "I love you," he gives her a big smooch. Now this super smarty is a therapy dog, too. He loves making kids in the hospital smile. His happy story is inspiring people all over the world, including his many fans on social media. He's also showing the world how important exercise and training is to dogs everywhere.

MR. PEEBLES

WHERE: SANTA ROSA, CALIFORNIA, U.S.A.

When two abandoned newborn puppies arrived at Sonoma County Animal Care and Control, rescuers went into action. Sadly, it was too late to save the tiny female. The little male didn't look good either, but he hung on. Rescue staff watched and waited and hoped. They celebrated when the precious pup showed signs of improvement. Soon he was well enough to move into a foster home. No one cared that he looked a little different. His missing teeth and crooked smile made him all the more lovable. But the sweet puppy still had a lot of healing and growing to do. His devoted foster mom bottle-fed the baby around the clock, snuggled him, and cared for his wounds. After months of care, Mr. Peebles made a full recovery. He rolled and played and acted silly like a healthy puppy should. He taught his caregivers a lot about getting through tough times and coming out smiling, no matter how many teeth you have. He was adopted into a loving home and spreads joy wherever he goes.

I ROCK ...
AND ROLL!

CASSIDY

WHERE: FORT LANGLEY, BRITISH COLUMBIA, CANADA

When TinyKittens Society found a sad nine-week-old kitten outdoors, nearly starved and suffering after a terrible injury to his back legs, staff members were shocked he was still alive. His legs needed to be amputated, but nothing could suppress this kitty's will to live. He refused to give up on life. His rescuers refused to give up on him. After his recovery, they constructed slings, splints, and eventually a set of mini-wheels to give his back end a lift and keep him mobile. All the while they documented his progress on social media. He had tons of fans! And the fans wanted to help. People from all over the world sent contraptions for his rescuers to try to help Cassidy's mobility. But nobody would have guessed that after seven months of intensive physical therapy, the miracle kitty would be able to get around on his own. Now Cassidy is a troublemaking youngster who loves to scamper around and tackle his housemates. And if he ever gets tired, he hitches a ride on his family's robotic vacuum cleaner.

HONEYBEE

WHERE: SEATTLE, WASHINGTON, U.S.A.

Honeybee the cat loves to stop and smell the flowers (and the moss, rocks, and even the weeds) when she goes hiking with her owners. But life wasn't always coming up roses for this adventurous feline. She was born in Fiji and was blind from birth. After she was rescued and cared for by a rescue group called Animals Fiji, an adoring American adopted her while on vacation. This cat has her challenges, but she doesn't sweat the small stuff or let it get in the way of having fun. She loves hiking and stopping to listen to the gurgle of a creek. If she gets tired, she rides on her human's shoulder for a while or catnaps in a special kitty sling. At home, she stays busy chilling with the four other cats in her family, chasing beetles, and eavesdropping on the neighbor's dog. No matter what she's doing, this girl just wants to show the world how great the life of a rescue cat—even one with a disability—can be.

Cats can't taste sweetness, but they can taste other flavors that humans can't.

JORDAN

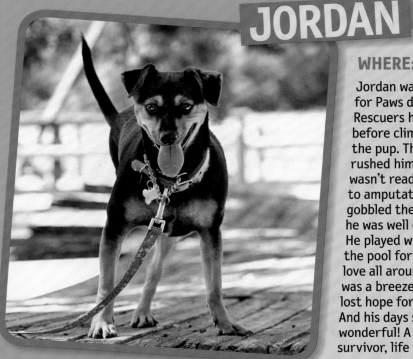

WHERE: LOS ANGELES, CALIFORNIA, U.S.A.

Jordan was in terrible shape when rescuers from Hope for Paws discovered him in an empty canal basin. Rescuers had to climb a ladder to get over a fence before climbing down into the drained ditch to reach the pup. They lifted him out in a basket on a rope and rushed him to the emergency vet. But resilient Jordan wasn't ready to give up. After lots of hugs, and surgery to amputate a leg, Jordan started feeling better. He gobbled the scrambled eggs his caregivers offered. Soon he was well enough to move into a loving foster home. He played with his frisky new foster friends. He swam in the pool for physical therapy. With friends and fun and love all around, learning how to operate on three legs was a breeze. Jordan may have lost a limb, but he never lost hope for a better day and a family to call his own. And his days soon were not only better, but downright wonderful! A loving family adopted Jordan. For this little survivor, life is now just one sunny day after another.

XENA

WHERE: JOHNS CREEK, GEORGIA, U.S.A.

Not all warriors start out brave and strong. When a homeless mutt was found collapsed and starving, rescuers at the DeKalb County Animal Services weren't sure this neglected puppy would make it. She weighed only four pounds (1.8 kg) and was in terrible shape. But Xena had a lot of fight left. The fragile pup survived one day and then another. She began to gain weight and thrive. When a mom on social media read about Xena's story, she felt an instant connection. Soon she brought her very shy son, an eight-year-old with autism, to meet the dog. The boy adored Xena, so his mom adopted her on the spot. Since then, Xena has had an incredible impact on her human boy. He smiles a lot more and communicates much more freely with those around him, thanks to Xena's attention and companionship. Now the pair are taking the world by storm, sharing the message about the power of pet adoption and fighting for better futures for animals everywhere. They call her Xena the Warrior Dog.

Xena was named the 2013 ASPCA Dog of the Year.

House cats have more than 30 muscles in their ears.

COLT

CANDY

CANDY AND COLT

WHERE: CLEVELAND, OHIO, U.S.A.

Before Candy and Colt were born, their mama was in need of a rescue. She was scared, pregnant, and homeless. Luckily, a girl named Harley found this lonesome mom. An animal lover, the girl had started an organization called Blankets Fur Beasties and collected comfort items for shelters. She also collected foster kitties! Harley and her mom rescued the mama kitty, whom they named Sugar, and took her to a small private shelter called Stay-A-While. There, she could have her babies safely. After Sugar's two tiny white kittens were born, Harley and her mom fostered the whole little family. The kittens, named Candy and Colt, learned to trust humans. One day, a pair of volunteers at the shelter adopted the two cute kittens. Now this little bit of double trouble is busy living happily ever after. Colt is a snuggle bunny and Candy likes to do her own thing. Two things they both love? Being carried around like babies and watching TV.

ÉCLAIR

WHERE: FRONT ROYAL, VIRGINIA, U.S.A.

This pretty pony pulled a cart in Baltimore, Maryland. But when her owner was evicted because of poor stable conditions, Éclair was sent to live at Days End Farm Horse Rescue. Other than needing to see an equine dentist and to get better-fitting shoes, Éclair wasn't in bad shape. But she did need a new home—and that's exactly what this gorgeous girl got. Her new owner adored her from first sight. Now Éclair is free to be herself—a curious, sassy pony who loves her home and her job carrying her owner on trail rides through the Virginia mountains. Éclair loves to snack on apples and gingersnap cookies and hang out with her friends in the pasture. Éclair may be a pony, but her owner says she's a real social butterfly.

BEFORE

AFTER

BRUISER

WHERE: NEW YORK, NEW YORK, U.S.A.

This formerly homeless Labrador retriever is one of the only dogs in the world with a nose highly trained to find wild tigers. The talented pup was rescued by a group that trains dogs to help scientists. In 2011, Bruiser joined an expedition to Bhutan in southern Asia to find out if there were any tigers living in the remote eastern end of the Himalaya mountains. Bruiser was in charge of sniffing out tiger poop. On the job in Bhutan, Bruiser put his nose to the ground and sniffed out his target much faster than the human team. He also taught them about the value of swim breaks! During his career, he has tracked other animals like jaguars in South America, Javan rhinos in Vietnam, and mountain lions and black bears in North America. Now retired, Bruiser lives in New York City and enjoys lots of naps and long walks in Central Park. But even in the city, his owner says Bruiser is always sniffing for tigers and jaguars.

A dog's sense of smell is 1,000 to 10,000,000 times better than that of a human!

WEE WEE

In France, humans use pigs to sniff out truffles.

WHERE: POOLESVILLE, MARYLAND, U.S.A.

Luckily for him, when a little piggy got stuck in a snowbank, a family driving by noticed the shivering pink lump. The Good Samaritans dug him out of the snow during a blizzard, brushed the ice from his ears, and wrapped him in a sweatshirt. Then they took him home for a warm bath and fed him bananas. Family members took turns sleeping with the snuggly piglet in the bathtub that night. Once the roads cleared, they delivered him to a fine forever home at Poplar Spring Animal Sanctuary. Now Wee Wee lives like a king. He devours piggy chow, lives with a BFF named Scooter (they wear matching sweaters), and even has a teddy bear and a special bed. What a lucky guy!

BANDIT AND CLYDE

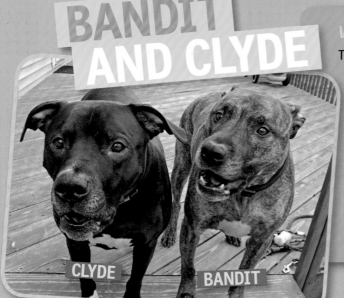

CLYDE

BANDIT

URBANDALE, IOWA, U.S.A.

The more the merrier, right? That's what Bandit's family said when they realized their very hugga-*bull* rescue dog's brother had been returned to the Animal Rescue League of Iowa. They had both been adopted as eight-week-old pit bull mix puppies. Then sweet Clyde's owner could no longer care for him. But Bandit's family could! They set up a doggie playdate to let the brothers get reacquainted. After a playful reunion, the family brought Clyde home forever, too. Now these dogs' days are on an endless loop of playing at the park, romping, squeezing into their mom's recliner for lap naps, and, of course, snacking on all the liver treats their mother will let them have. There's a whole lot of brotherly love in this family.

SALEM

WHERE: **LEXINGTON, KENTUCKY, U.S.A.**

Salem went the distance to show his family just how much he loved them. Elizabeth Ober adopted Salem from an animal shelter on a military base in 2004. In the years following, Salem moved with his family to Italy, Texas, and North Dakota. The affectionate house cat entertained them with his signature "howl." But during their last move, from an apartment to a house eight miles (13 km) away, skittish Salem bolted out the front door and didn't come back. For months, his owners put out food and shelter at the door to their old apartment, but no luck. The whole family missed Salem terribly. Two months later, a skinny black cat showed up at the door of their new house. Elizabeth didn't believe it could be Salem, but then she recognized his signature howl. Their dog greeted the cat with a friendly lick, and a vet later confirmed it—this was Salem! Somehow Salem had crossed two busy highways, passed through miles of farmland, and picked the right house in a huge subdivision. Salem seemed happy to be home. Like a typical cat, he waltzed inside like he owned the place, and that was that.

Adult cats only meow to communicate with humans.

BRAVE AND DARING HEROES

It's a bird! It's a plane! It's a superhero to the rescue! Meet these pumped-up pets who are ready to save the day.

NUDGE USES A SPECIAL "KITTY DOOR" TO GET IN AND OUT.

NUDGE

WHERE: JAMESVILLE, NEW YORK, U.S.A.

A stray cat had been hanging out at the edge of his field for a while, but every time Nic Pascal would approach, the cat would run away. He set out food and waited. Finally, one day, the cat let him scoop her up and take her to the vet. After checking her out, the vet guessed the fluffy kitty to be between 18 and 24 months old. He also noticed that her top front teeth were worn down to nubs. She might have been eating the bark off trees because she was so hungry. Nic took the ravenous cat home and gave her everything she needed, including tons of food. To thank her new family, the cat gave them lots of affection— Nic's wife named her Nudge because of her head-butting habits. Nudge settled into her new life and loved her family. One night, Nudge woke up Nic and wouldn't let him go back to sleep. He pushed her off the bed but she kept coming back and jumping on his chest. Finally he got up. That's when he noticed black smoke billowing out of the garage and into the house. He yelled to his wife and called 911. Firefighters arrived in time to save the family. After the ordeal, the fire chief had a piece of advice for the homeowner: Never let that cat go!

At the organization's 12th Annual Real Heroes Breakfast, the American Red Cross of Central New York awarded Nudge their "Hero of the Year."

BELLA

WHERE: DECATUR, TEXAS, U.S.A.

When a heat lamp malfunctioned in her barn and started a fire, Bella the pony acted fast to protect her two-week-old foal, Butterscotch. Bella backed the baby into a corner and used her own body to shield Butterscotch from the flames.

Even though she was badly burned, Bella was still protecting her foal when firefighters discovered them. Butterscotch only had a few minor burns, thanks to her mom's heroic actions. But Bella was covered with burns all over her body and suffering from smoke inhalation. Her owners sadly couldn't afford the vet care, but the Humane Society of North Texas stepped in to care for the ponies. Bella's injuries were serious. She nearly died, but this supermom fought for her life so she could continue to care for her foal.

Months later, Bella has recovered. A Humane Society volunteer adopted the pair of ponies. Now they live on a homey 40-acre (16.2-ha) ranch. Bella still cares for Butterscotch, who's now two years old. Bella is retired, but when Butterscotch gets a little older, the spirited and friendly young pony will go to work as an ambassador for the Humane Society, visiting schools and educating the public about the importance of caring for animals.

In the United States, about three million homeless pets get adopted into forever homes every year.

JETHRO

WHERE: BOULDER, COLORADO, U.S.A.

During his days at the Boulder Humane Society, Jethro the homeless mutt made friends with other dogs, cats, ducks, geese, and goats. When he was adopted, his new home in the mountains included lots of room to run and long, happy jaunts outdoors.

One day he came home with a tiny orphaned baby cottontail rabbit in his mouth. Jethro's owner wondered if the dog had killed the bunny by accident. Then Jethro burped and dropped the baby bunny at his owner's feet. She was drenched in slobber but unharmed. Jethro stood there until his owner understood that the baby bunny needed caring for. His owner named her Bunny and put her in a box with a blanket and some carrots, celery, and water. Over the next two weeks, Jethro's owner cared for the bunny until she was ready to go back outside. Jethro refused to leave the bunny's side, except to eat and take short walks. He even slept next to Bunny's box. And a year later, Jethro brought home a bird who needed help. This gentle giant was a real lifesaver!

JETHRO IS A ROTTWEILER MIX LIKE THE ONE PICTURED HERE.

SCRAPPY

WHERE: LONDON, ENGLAND, U.K.

Scrappy the cat was adopted as a kitten and given a safe forever home by his devoted owners. But now at 18, he's a bit of a cat of a different color. Although this cuddly kitten was born with a black coat, white spots started to appear on his dark fur at age 7. Those white patches kept showing up. Today spotty Scrappy has a unique salt and pepper blend of white and black fur. His family believes he may have a condition called vitiligo, which causes a loss of color in the skin. That means that Scrappy might turn entirely white over time. But otherwise, Scrappy's vet says he's a perfect pattern of health, even with his unusual look. And his owners think it just makes him look even more handsome!

SCRAPPY WAS BORN AN ALL-BLACK CAT LIKE THIS ONE.

Black cats are often associated with luck.

CHINO

WHERE: LINTHICUM, MARYLAND, U.S.A.

When Chino arrived at Days End Farm Horse Rescue, he was nearly starved to death and in terrible shape. His former owners had seriously neglected his care. He was in so much pain upon getting off the horse trailer, he wouldn't stop grinding his teeth. He ended up in intensive care and struggled to survive. He had a long recovery, but this survivor went from bad shape to beautiful with the rescue's care. When a girl visited to see about adopting a horse, she couldn't take her eyes off Chino. It was love at first sight. Chino joined up with the family's other rescue horses and began his new life as a pampered pet. He loves going for trail rides, hanging out in the barn with his girl, competing at horse shows, and even swimming in the Chesapeake Bay.

E.B.

WHERE: STATEN ISLAND, NEW YORK, U.S.A.

Rabbits live in a network of burrows called a warren.

When a domestic silver lop-eared rabbit was found abandoned in New York, a concerned rabbit lover snapped a picture and posted it on social media with a plea for help. The picture was shared over and over. Experienced Texas-based rabbit rescuer Diana Leggett saw pictures of the scared bunny many states away and hopped into action. The founder of WildRescue, Inc./ Rabbit Rescue, Diana worried that a cold dark night was falling 1,600 miles (2,575 km) away and that the rabbit was in danger. She reposted and shared the pictures on social media. Then something clicked. She heard from a bunny-loving friend in New York who was minutes away from the lop's location. Within an hour, the indoor pet was safely in a pet carrier and back inside. Diana posted an update and people all over the country cheered. As for the rabbit (named E.B., short for Easter Bunny), after a trip to the vet the next day, she was adopted by a rabbit lover who had followed the story online. We don't "like" this social media story, we love it!

KIAH

NEVER FEAR—
KIAH'S HERE!

Before you start to train your dog, figure out what motivates him or her, like a treat, a stick, or a ball.

WHERE: POUGHKEEPSIE, NEW YORK, U.S.A.

This happy hound with a soaring spirit started out as a pound pup in a Texas animal shelter, after she was found in a parking lot abandoned and abused. With help from Animal Farm Foundation (an organization in New York that helps pit bull–type dogs) and Universal K9, she was trained and placed with the City of Poughkeepsie Police Department. Now she's using her loads of energy and smarts (and her nose) to fight crime as a drug-sniffing police dog. She's also trained to use her sniffer to track missing humans. Day to day, she and her partner, Officer Justin Bruzgul, patrol the streets, keeping their town safe. Super energetic, agile, and affectionate, K9 Kiah's also helping spread the word that pit bull–type dogs can do the same law enforcement work as purebred, purpose-bred dogs. 10-4, Officer Kiah—good dog!

IT LOOKS JUST LIKE ME!

MR. PICKLES

WHERE: SEATTLE, WASHINGTON, U.S.A.

Mr. Pickles the cat always seemed to know he was a therapy cat at heart. The smart boy had figured out how to navigate the automatic doors of a nearby retirement center. He often made himself right at home. He liked visiting with the residents and warming himself by the fire. The residents loved him, too. He had a way of brightening their days. They liked to pet and cuddle the cute cat. But one day, Mr. Pickles was left homeless. His owner had to move from the neighborhood, and was not allowed to bring Mr. Pickles with him. Luckily, Mr. Pickles had options. The nursing home adopted the friendly cat. Now, when Mr. Pickles isn't busy providing purrs, head-butts, and snuggles to his many friends, this terrific tabby can be found relaxing in the garden, going to church on Sundays in the chapel, and attending meetings with the residents. One thing he never misses? Movie night.

LADY MARY

WHERE: RIO RANCHO, NEW MEXICO, U.S.A.

When a very sick guinea pig needed help, Haven for Hamsters, a rescue organization that focuses on pets small enough to fit in a pocket, got a call. The little pet was suffering from a bad infection and a head wound. She couldn't walk or eat without help. But her patient rescuers helped her learn to walk again. They also hand-fed her until she could feed herself. Two other residents at the refuge, Gigi and Gino the rabbits, took her under their "wings" and helped her recover. Named Lady Mary, the guinea pig recovered so well she started to come when her rescuer called. Lucky for Lady Mary, this pocket pet will stay forever at Haven for Hamsters. After all, it's where her best friends live.

Guinea pigs can walk immediately after birth.

PUDDING

WHERE: STURGEON BAY, WISCONSIN, U.S.A.

When Amy Jung and her son visited the Door County Humane Society, they hadn't planned on adopting a cat. But after meeting Pudding, they couldn't leave without him. They had only just met, but he already felt like family. That night, he would become more like family than they could ever expect. Jung had a dangerous diabetic seizure in her sleep. The clever kitty knew something was wrong. Pudding leapt up on her chest and bopped his owner on the face. When she didn't move, he gently nipped her nose. Jung woke up, but couldn't move or speak. That's when Pudding ran to wake up Jung's son, somehow opening a closed door to get to him. When her son woke up and realized his mother was in trouble, he gave her a lifesaving injection. Without it, she would have died. But thanks to heroic Pudding, everyone is safe and happy. Jung feels lucky to have a big, fuzzy guardian angel.

LANCE

WHERE: RAJASTHAN, INDIA

When Animal Aid Unlimited heard about a working donkey injured and abandoned on the street, rescuers took action. The donkey could barely walk but was willing and trusting enough to go with his rescuers for treatment. Two months later, after surgery and loads of TLC, the donkey (named Lance to honor his courageous knight-like demeanor) retired to the Bonnie Christopher Forever Home for Donkeys. These days Lance is strong and healthy. His days are full of peace and friends, as well as snacks like buckets of tasty grain and fresh hay. He won't ever have to pull a cart or carry a heavy load again.

MY NAME MIGHT BE COMET, BUT I'M REALLY A STAR!

Because of his name, Comet has a NASA ID tag!

COMET

WHERE: DUNEDIN, FLORIDA, U.S.A.

When Comet was a puppy, it seemed like no one wanted him. The tiny Jack Russell terrier had been adopted twice but returned to the shelter both times. Shelter workers feared that no one was willing to put in the work and care for him properly. But that all changed when Comet was spotted by a dog lover named Brendan. Brendan adopted Comet and immediately set to correcting the feisty pup's unruly behavior. It took years, but the two became inseparable—and Comet came to display model behavior. Even better, Comet was soon a model himself! Brendan worked at the Home Shopping Network, and because Comet was so well behaved (and adorable), he became the network's go-to dog for modeling pet products on television. And when he wasn't working, Comet would sit in meetings or nap under Brendan's desk. These days, 17-year-old Comet is retired from modeling. Even so, the pampered pooch remains on his best behavior—and, of course, spends his time snacking, snuggling, and sleeping.

BAMBI

WHERE: HARTFORD, CONNECTICUT, U.S.A.

A tiny kitten hid in a garage, homeless and alone. The kind person who found her delivered the kitty to Smart Animal Rescue in Spring, Texas. Her caregivers soon noticed the kitten (now named Bambi) was deaf. Around the same time, a couple who lived on the East Coast visited an online pet adoption site and checked the search box for "special needs" cats. The couple was looking for a deaf kitten. They were deaf, too. One click led to another, and soon they discovered the listing for the little deaf kitten. Soon the kitten was on her way to Connecticut on a bus full of rescued pets. While they waited for her arrival, one of Bambi's new owners began teaching a little sign language to one of their other cats, Bobcat. She hoped that this would help them communicate to their new kitty. Soon Bobcat understood the hand signal that meant if he approached, he would get a treat. When Bambi arrived, she followed Bobcat's lead. Soon she understood the signal, too. It wasn't long before the cats had learned even more sign language, like the signs for sit and stay. Bambi has even learned to sign back! When her owner makes the sign for "play," Bambi stretches up and taps her owner's hand with her paw. That means she wants her owner to get a wad of crumpled paper and play fetch. Well played, Bambi!

American Sign Language is the third most common language in the United States.

SUPER-SWEET SENIORS

Many gray-muzzled senior dogs and elderly cats are overlooked in shelters. But often senior animals have so much to give, like patience and lots of cuddles. Read these stories of how these stars shine, no matter their age.

STELLA AND CLAIRE

STELLA

CLAIRE

WHERE: WILMINGTON, DELAWARE, U.S.A.

Everybody loves a puppy, but senior dogs make great pets, too. It's hard to understand how someone could surrender a pet during their old age, but it does happen. Fortunately there are rescuers, like the volunteers at Senior Dog Haven and Hospice, who specialize in caring for many homeless, elderly animals. Like Stella: At 18 years old, this fantastic frosty-faced lady found herself in a shelter because she could no longer hear or walk up the stairs. Heartbroken shelter staff called the rescue and begged for help. The sweet, gentle Lab was shaking and terrified. Her story might have come to an end at the shelter, but instead one of the rescue's foster families opened up their hearts and their home to this deserving old girl. Another time, Senior Dog Haven and Hospice went into action when they heard about a 20-year-old poodle mix who had been dropped at the shelter. She had heart problems. She had eye problems. But she also still had a lot of love to give. Now in a comfy home, quiet Claire will be snuggled and cherished for all her days. Her foster mom says 21 is going to be Claire's best year yet.

CLEO

All cats were considered sacred in ancient Egypt.

WHERE: SURREY, ENGLAND, U.K.

When 89-year-old cat lover Nancy Cowen couldn't live on her own any longer, she moved to a nursing home. Neighbors agreed to take in her beloved cat, Cleo. But devoted Cleo had other plans. Nancy had taken the fluffy stray in off the streets about 10 years before. Somehow the clever feline made her way more than a mile (1.6 km) to the nursing home even though she'd never been there. Soon, staff at the place noticed a Persian cross hanging around outside. Cold, hungry, and with matted hair, Cleo spent three weeks peering in windows and sleeping on a patio table outside her owner's room. The staff thought she was a stray cat. One night an employee picked up the cat. Nancy opened her window and said, "That looks like my cat!" That's when Cleo scrambled inside for a purr-filled reunion. Now the pair is living happily ever after at the nursing home. Both Cleo and Nancy have a home there for life.

HARLEY

WHERE: BERTHOUD, COLORADO, U.S.A.

This one-eyed Chihuahua was rescued after spending 10 sad years in a puppy mill, a place that breeds puppies in great quantities and often in poor conditions. Now he's a world-famous spokesdog who spreads the word about the hazards of puppy mills. Before his rescue, Harley was abused, injured, and left in terrible conditions. When he was rescued and given a forever home, the poor dog was only given a few months to live. But six-pound (2.7-kg) Harley never gave up on life. He fully recovered and lived life to the fullest. Harley was missing an eye, and had deformed legs, among other medical issues from the years spent at the puppy mill. Still, this little spokesdog served as the adorable furry face of the "Harley to the Rescue" campaign, which raises money for the National Mill Dog Rescue. Harley has since passed on, but he spent his time going on rescue missions and making appearances at schools and events. His rescue campaign has helped save more than 500 dogs from puppy mills, and has raised more than half a million dollars! This little road-tripping warrior put all his might into barking out for other dogs who need help.

I HAVE THE NOSE OF A BUD-HOUND.

WACHA

WHERE: NEW YORK, NEW YORK, U.S.A.

Talk about rags to riches—this rescued star now helps host a TV show in the Big Apple. Rescue group See Spot Rescued plucked this perfect pup out of a crowded shelter in West Virginia. The sporty spotted pup made the trip to New Jersey, where celebrity TV host Andy Cohen adopted the beautiful beagle mix. Now the pampered pup lives it up in the city, rubbing shoulders with other celebrity pups, walking the city streets with a professional dog walker, and making regular appearances on TV to please his eager fans.

Nearly half of all homes in the United States have a dog, about a third of homes have a cat.

FROSTY

AFTER

WHERE: ELYRIA, OHIO, U.S.A.

When an exhausted and lost kitten collapsed, cold and wet, on the road, dipping temperatures soon caused him to freeze to ice on the side of the road. A passing driver spotted the kitten and stopped to help.

The kitten's caregivers at the Friendship Animal Protective League weren't sure if their tiny patient would live. His frostbitten tail had to be amputated. The ice had badly damaged the pads on his feet. He had an infection in both eyes and a bad cold. But after a few days of care and plenty of food, he started running around, getting into trouble, and chasing toys like most kittens do. Shelter staff gave him a chill new name: Frosty.

The tough kitty soon made a full recovery. Best of all, Frosty was adopted into a warm, loving family of his own.

BEFORE

MOOSE
AND MOLLY

WHERE: ROCKVILLE, MARYLAND, U.S.A.

When a massive mastiff was found tied to a tree, rescuers from Mutts Matter Rescue gave him shelter and care. Not long after, this giant hunk of love found his forever home. His new family had a spacious house for all of his handsome 180 pounds (81.6 kg) to spread out in, and a big backyard (oh, and lots of food!). Not long after, this gentle giant's family opted to foster another homeless dog so Moose could have a playmate. That's when little Molly moved in. The pocket-size pit had been found abandoned in the woods and was very sick. After she started to feel better, she and Moose loved to play tug-of-war for hours and then crash on the couch together. Moose and Molly were such great pals that the family adopted her, too. It didn't even matter that Moose was XXXL and Molly was a tiny lady. Sadly, Moose passed away in 2015. But Molly is still living the good life. This petite bundle of mischief and her humans still miss Moose, but Molly keeps her owners entertained. They say her tail never stops wagging—she might be small but she has a moose-size personality!

MOLLY

MOOSE

If humans varied in size as much as dogs, the smallest would be 2 feet (0.6 m) tall and the tallest would be about 31 feet (9.4 m) tall.

ROSCOE

WHERE: ELLIS COUNTY, OKLAHOMA, U.S.A.

A police dog named Roscoe started his journey as a stray taken off the streets by the Nebraska Humane Society. The dog had a lot of spunk and smiles, but many potential adopters passed him by. A dog behavioral expert at the shelter named Dawn Thrapp noticed Roscoe's love of chasing balls and toys. That energy and focus made her think Roscoe would be highly motivated to learn. She called experienced law enforcement dog trainer Ed Van Buren. Could he help save this dog with no options? Ed agreed to give Roscoe a try. Roscoe excelled in his training work, easily learning the skills a dog must master to work in drug detection: odor memorization, searching skills, the ability to point out found objects, and the ability to concentrate even around distractions. Roscoe impressed his trainer with his focus, enthusiasm, and gentle nature. Thankfully, the peachy pup's hard work paid off. A police department in Oklahoma gave him a job. His partner, Deputy TJ Tyler, gave Roscoe something even better: a forever home.

Dogs pant up to 300 times a minute.

AFTER

BEFORE

GISELE

WHERE: ATHENS, GREECE

Gisele the miniature horse was born in a ramshackle pen at a gas station on a touristy Greek island. Her mother died when she was a foal. After eight years of living in isolated and unhealthy conditions, Gisele was starving, unhappy, and sick. The founder of Gentle Carousel Miniature Therapy Horses heard about the situation and went into action. He convinced the owner to surrender her, then organized a van and a boat that would allow a miniature horse aboard. Gisele had never left her pen or worn a halter, but she let her rescuer lead her to safety. After a 10-hour boat ride, the little horse was on her way. She hadn't seen another horse since her mother died, but Gisele whinnied with excitement to see the herd of miniature horses at her new home. It took a while for Gisele to regain her health, but she did so in the company of her new horsey BFFs. Now she's a therapy horse, too. She visits senior citizens and children with special needs. Give this little sweetie a blue ribbon!

MEATHEAD

WHERE: EVANSVILLE, INDIANA, U.S.A.

Stray cats have a hard life. This was true for a nearly toothless stray who spent his days hungry and alone—even in the cold winter. When concerned resident Caroline Hagedorn started feeding him, she named him Meathead because of his big head. She called him Meatie for short. At first, he'd run away if he saw her. But eventually Meatie felt comfortable enough to sit on her front steps, even though he would hiss if she got too close. Caroline set up a cozy shelter on her porch with an irresistible electric blanket so he could get warm during the winter. Meatie must have liked it, because he spent about 20 hours a day in the comfy place. A year later, Meatie finally let his kind human touch him. She guessed he was about 10 years old. He was still afraid, but would climb out to cuddle if she sat still for long enough. Little by little, Meatie learned to trust his human. Trust turned to love. For the rest of his life he knew his name and waited every day for his adoptive human to come home from work. They hung out together for four years. He loved to lay on her head and purr, she says, sounding like a giant lawnmower. He loved to eat the soft food she fed him. His human credits Meatie for showing her how tough and cold life can be for a stray cat.

Cats communicate using at least 16 known "cat words."

CALI

WHERE: NEW SOUTH WALES, AUSTRALIA

As a puppy, little Bungee the rescue puppy had the cutest wrinkly face and most amazing yellow eyes. But she still didn't have a forever home. Her foster mom, a volunteer with a rescue called Fetching Dogs, knew that shelter dogs often look sad or scared in their photos, and that this can make it tough for them to find new homes. So she decided to set up a fancy photo shoot to capture Bungee's true playful personality ... and her supercute face! Bungee got to lounge in the grass and snack on dog treats while the camera clicked away. The photo shoot worked! Bungee's glamour shots caught the eye of an adoptive family who fell in love with her at first sight. They renamed her "Cali." Since then, the little canine princess has been treated like royalty. She loves to curl up on the bed and nap, wrestle with her many doggie pals, and most of all loves to tag along with her older brother—Spencer the cat. As for her family, they are forever grateful for the photograph that led them to their precious fur baby. And they still think her face is the super-cutest of all.

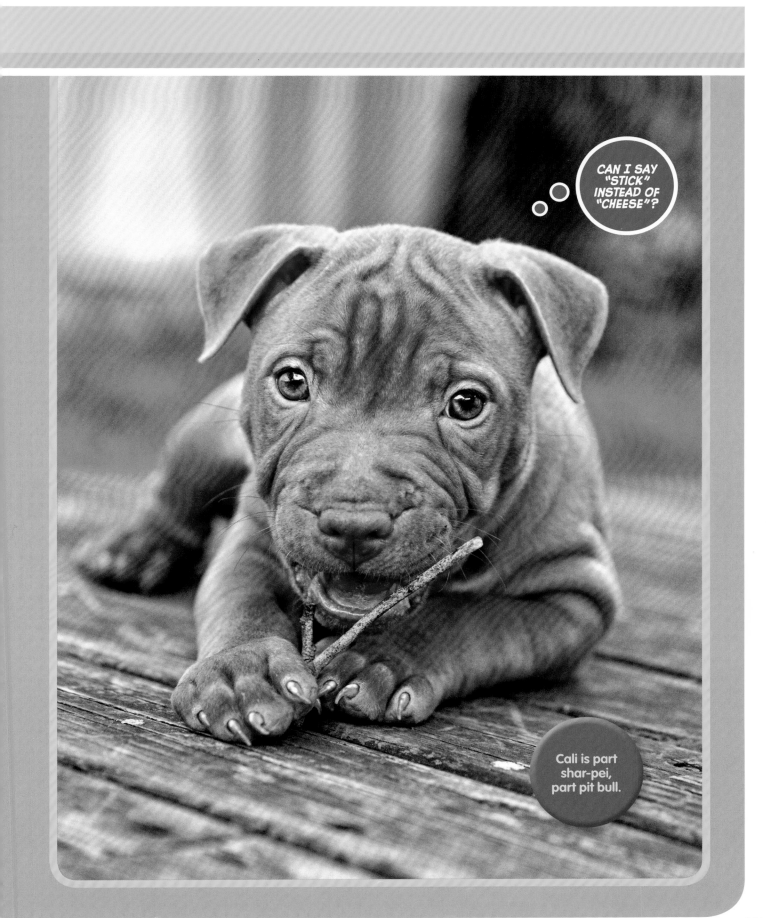

A goat's beard is called a goatee.

JIMMY BARNES

WHERE: VICTORIA, AUSTRALIA

When a beautiful goat was in danger, rescue groups Five Freedoms Animal Rescue and Edgar's Mission went into action. The working goat had been owned by someone who set him out on their property to keep wild berries under control. But when he became homeless, neighbors didn't appreciate his grazing ways. It seemed like the goat was out of luck. He was scared of humans and hard to handle. But rescuers tracked the goat, tranquilized him, and carried him to safety. They treated him with great kindness, care, and a lot of his favorite Weetabix treats. Now this glorious goat no longer fears humans. He has the run of his forever home at Edgar's Mission, where he and his friends roam free for life in a place called Goatville. His favorite part of his new home? Kidding around on top of "Goat Mountain," a custom playground for goats.

PANCAKE

WHERE: LOUISVILLE, KENTUCKY, U.S.A.

One day, a woman named Vicky Vinch heard about a dog named Pancake who needed a new home. The poor pup had been abused before she was rescued. Vicky saw a picture, fell in love, and decided to adopt her. Even though Pancake now had a new home, the abuse she went through left her scared and unsure. In her new house, she sat in the corner and shivered. She refused to play or go near people. But soon, with lots of patience and love, this sweet little flapjack realized she was safe. Little by little she began to play with other dogs and give the humans around her a try. But that's not all: When this sweetheart's wounds healed, Vicky trained her to be a service dog. Vicky has serious balance issues because of a medical disability, but Pancake stays by her side to help out and keep her steady. When she's not serving as her owner's devoted companion and helper, she loves a good romp at the dog park. Lucky for this girl, now her life's a piece of cake!

LUCKY

FOR MY NEXT ACT, I'LL MAKE SOME CHOW DISAPPEAR!

WHERE: LONGMONT, COLORADO, U.S.A.

When a 650-pound (295-kg) pig fell off a truck cruising down the highway, was it bad luck or a James Bond–like escape strategy? The poor piggy was probably on his way to be sold for meat. Instead, he was found and rescued by a police officer. The officer called Weld County Animal Control, who then contacted a sanctuary for abandoned pigs called Hog Haven Farm. Lucky was given that name for a reason—he was really lucky to survive falling out of a truck onto a highway with no serious injuries. He did have a few scrapes and cuts on his ample backside, but he healed fast. Now this hoggy Houdini has the best possible life. He loves to run, play with sticks, and have his big, floppy ears scratched. His bestie is a potbellied pig named Hamlet. They love to snuggle and nap in the sunshine. Lucky's a big pig with a lot of personality.

EXCALIBUR

WHERE: VICTORIA, AUSTRALIA

Excalibur is a rescued rooster with a puppy dog personality. He's gentle and kind and loves to cuddle with his human friends. But life wasn't always so sweet for this fancy feathered friend. Before he was rescued by an animal sanctuary called Edgar's Mission, he was used for cockfighting. That's a cruel and illegal sport in which roosters are made to fight, sometimes with sharp spurs attached to their legs. This gentle guy came into the rescue blind in one eye and with a broken beak. But Excalibur's days no longer include fear and pain. Instead of fighting, he focuses on keeping the peace among his pals at the rescue—especially when his plucky duck friend Miss Puddleduck and a calf named Buffy get a little rowdy.

Chickens chat with more than 24 different "words," including peeps and purrs.

SNUFFLES

WHERE: GLASGOW, SCOTLAND, U.K.

Snuffles the rescue dog uses his nose like most dogs do, but there's nothing typical about how his sniffer looks. His schnoz has an unusual split in the middle that makes him look like he has an extra nose! This is because his nostrils formed separately instead of fusing together like on most dogs. This rare condition is called a cleft nose. Snuffles was taken in by rescuers at the Dogs Trust Rehoming Centre when his owners couldn't care for him. Because he looked a bit unusual to most people, it took a little while for Snuffles to find an adopter. But this super sniffer eventually found a perfect home. Best of all, his forever family loves him just the way he is—which is nothing to sneeze at.

NOW MY LIFE IS TWICE AS NICE!

TARA

WHERE: LOS ANGELES, CALIFORNIA, U.S.A.

When a stray kitten followed a family home from the park one day, they gave her a home. But they couldn't have predicted how Tara would one day pay them back. When a dog attacked the cat's four-year-old human brother, this heroic house cat rushed to the scene and defended the boy with her bare claws. Forget 911, this little tiger had the situation under control. She chased the dog away, then circled back to check on her boy. After the potentially *cat*-astrophic incident, Tara's owner said the terrific tabby acted like it was no big deal.

CELEBRITY RESCUES

Call the *pup*-arazzi—these pets are spectacular! Check out these super-sweet stars who started out home-less and ended up as the cat's meow.

LIL BUB

WHERE: BLOOMINGTON, INDIANA, U.S.A.

Rescued as a feral kitten with special needs, this superstar kitty has a rare and extreme case of dwarfism, which means she'll always look like a kitten. But no one wanted to adopt this needy kitty ... except a man who took one look at the tiny little orphan and called her Bub. She started purring like crazy and fell asleep on his shoulder. Bub's new owner took her home, intro-duced her to his other rescue cats, and took care of her. Despite her unique condition, Lil Bub is a healthy cat and per-fectly happy. She's also very busy. With help from her owner, Lil Bub has published a book, become one of the most followed cats on social media, given interviews on national television, and starred in a documentary. Lil Bub has always had a sunny outlook on life. Now that she's a star, she just keeps on shining.

Lil Bub has helped raise more than $300,000 for needy animals.

Tuna adores staying in hotels when he travels.

TUNA

WHERE: LOS ANGELES, CALIFORNIA, U.S.A.

There's nothing fishy about this Fido's fame. Found on the side of a road in San Diego, California, Tuna found his forever home thanks to a rescue organization in Los Angeles. At first, Tuna's owner took pictures of him daily to document his adorable Chihuahua-dachshund look and the sensationally silly faces he loved to make. Then she created a social media account for her precious—and often cartoonish—pup. Within a few years, his fan following has grown to more than 1.8 million people! Tuna makes his fans smile. He makes them laugh. He has been the subject of a book, inspired merchandise, and has become a spokes-pooch for animal rescue everywhere.

MILLIE

WHERE: LOS ANGELES, CALIFORNIA, U.S.A.

When rescuers found a homeless four-year-old basset hound scavenging for scraps outside a restaurant, they brought the pretty girl back to the San Gabriel Valley Humane Society for a makeover and a meal. They named her Millie. It wasn't long before superstar actor George Clooney and his wife, Amal, made their way into the shelter. They'd seen Millie online and couldn't resist her sweet face and her long, soft ears. After a successful introduction to another dog in the family, Millie was adopted. Then, just like that, little miss homeless Millie joined the Clooney clan and became an instant celeb herself.

BAGEL

WHERE: LOS ANGELES, CALIFORNIA, U.S.A.

A rescue cat named Bagel doesn't wear sunglasses to be cool—she wears them to protect her eyes. Because she was born without eyelids, her adoptive owner came up with the idea to create some cat goggles and even decorated them for her sweet kitty. At first, Bagel didn't love her custom eyewear. But she soon adjusted, and now proudly rocks her gorgeous eye gear. Bagel's unique needs go beyond her eyewear—her body has trouble adjusting to colder temperatures, so she also has a coats, sweaters, and capes to keep her toasty warm. It's a good thing Bagel has a lot of fancy clothes. She's made headlines as a fashionista and uses her fame to raise awareness about pet adoption. She can often be found posing on the red carpet or appearing at countless "meet and greet" fund-raisers for charity. Above all, Bagel hopes her fame will encourage others to adopt super awesome special needs cats who make *purr*-fect pets.

FORGET THE CAT'S PAJAMAS—I HAVE A WHOLE WARDROBE.

OTTO AND BIRDIE

WHERE: WASHINGTON, D.C., U.S.A.

When adorable Otto first moved into his forever home, the wire-haired Irish wolfhound mix enjoyed long snoozes and toys. But the life of an older rescue dog is not always easy. Otto had spent a lot of his younger years in a crate. Whenever his new family left the house, he got very scared about being left behind. Once he hurt himself trying to get out of his crate. He also did a lot of loud, lonesome howling, which annoyed the neighbors. Devoted to making Otto feel better, his new owners tried everything, with no luck. Finally, they wondered if a canine companion might help Otto. So, they went back to the same rescue they adopted Otto from—Lucky Dog Animal Rescue—and found a mighty little pooch with kind eyes, big ears, and a huge heart. The family fell in love and named her Birdie. In her new home, Birdie took charge immediately and Otto could finally relax. Birdie soothed his nerves and babysat the big guy whenever the family had to go out. These days, Otto doesn't worry about much. He and Birdie snuggle, sleep, and snack together. When their owners come home from being out, Birdie runs to find Otto then barks at him as if to announce, "They're home! They're home!"

Puppies of large breeds have big, oversize paws that they have to grow into.

TYLER

WHERE: WASHINGTON, D.C., U.S.A.

Tyler has special boots to wear when he hikes in the snow.

When Tyler the Labrador/Great Pyrenees mix was rescued from the woods of West Virginia, he was starving and scared. But that didn't put a damper on his love for people, or slow his passion for the outdoors! Rescued by a loving couple in Washington, D.C., Tyler made it clear that despite his rough beginning, he was not afraid to go back in the woods. Tyler not only loved to go hiking, but also joined his human parents on camping and even backpacking trips. Not even the snow could stop him— he simply wrapped up in warm winter gear and trekked on. When Tyler wasn't busy being active, the happy hound was eager to display his mischievous side. He would often hide treats around his house, including in the fireplace and potted plants! He also worked as a therapy dog, visiting sick children in hospitals and doing tricks to make them laugh. These days, now that Tyler is older, he causes fewer shenanigans, but still loves nature. He spends his time relaxing in the sun, fishing in a nearby creek, and generally reminding his owners to see the good in life.

CALLIE AND DEVLIN

WHERE: DES MOINES, IOWA, U.S.A.

When Callie arrived at the Animal Rescue League of Iowa, an old injury that hadn't healed properly meant one of her legs had to be amputated. At about the same time, another small, stray kitten arrived at the shelter. Named Devlin by shelter staff, this kitty needed his tail amputated. Afterward, Callie and Devlin arrived in a cozy foster home, where they recovered together. Finding placements for homeless animals can be hard when the animals have special needs because they need extra care. But months after Devlin and Callie first arrived at the shelter, a wonderful family took them home together forever. Now these cats are free to live life to the fullest. For Callie and Devlin, being special needs led to an extra special friendship!

LEALA

WHERE: NEW SOUTH WALES, AUSTRALIA

Leala started life as a breeding dog. But when she got too old to have puppies, the breeder didn't want her anymore. Luckily, a kind family took her in, not knowing just how much she would repay them. Leala was enjoying a cookout with her humans when her family's toddler wandered off and nearly drowned in a nearby dam. All alone with the boy, Leala tried to help. When this rescue rover couldn't get the boy out herself, she raced to get help. The boy's father, alerted by Leala, arrived and pulled him out of the water. Soon the boy was on his way to the hospital in a helicopter. He recovered after the big scare. This quick-thinking hero dog saved her boy's life. Her reward? A lifetime of steaks and loads of love from her very grateful family.

TALK ABOUT BEING THE TEACHER'S PET!

NIGEL

WHERE: SILVER SPRING, MARYLAND, U.S.A.

As the humane educator for the Humane Rescue Alliance, Debbie Duel has helped lots of wonderful pets find their forever families. But when she was searching for a rescue dog for her family, she had trouble finding the right match. Debbie needed someone who would be good with kids, good with other animals, and comfortable going into the classrooms where she teaches kids about the humane treatment of animals. Finally, a young black Labrador retriever was brought to the Washington Humane Society shelter. The sweet pup had spent a long time chained in a yard with very little to eat, but he was wiggly and loving with a constantly wagging tail. He was perfect: Debbie fell in love with Nigel and adopted him. For the next 10 years, Nigel helped Debbie teach. Together, they encouraged kids to be kind, compassionate, and respectful to animals. These days Nigel is retired and devotes his days to hanging out with his adoring family. A-plus, Nigel!

ARE WE THERE YET?

A dog's nose-print can be used to identify it, the same way we use fingerprints.

HENRY

WHERE: MILL VALLEY, CALIFORNIA, U.S.A.

Lights, camera, action! As a puppy, Henry the shepherd mix was scooped up by animal control on the streets of Merced, California. Sheltered by Rocket Dog Rescue, he was then adopted by Caroline Kraus, a woman on a mission to make a film about the treatment of animals. She had seen a text with a photo of the scared, four-month-old puppy who was about to be euthanized. Caroline rushed to adopt him. Once he got settled in his new home, the young dog emerged as super smart, alert, and funny—the perfect partner for an epic road trip she had planned. Now, the dynamic duo are traveling the country documenting the people and animals they encounter along the way. They camp for a week at a time in state parks. Henry waits patiently while Caroline interviews people on film. Henry's made a lot of friends along the way—some humans and a lot of canines who love his passion for roughhousing, exploring, and playing chase. He also loves to roll in the parks' finest thick grasses. If it's cold out, Caroline swaddles Henry in blankets in the tent to keep him warm on his traveling dog bed. She also adds warm water to his kibble to warm him up from the inside. Henry seems to love his adopted mom's mission. He loves the idea of making the world a better place for animals all around. That's a wrap!

WHAT YOU CAN DO TO HELP

Pwdditat
Page 41

GARY WEITZMAN

DVM, MPH, CAWA
San Diego Humane Society

Every year, more than seven million animals find their way into shelters in the United States. This is an enormous number. At my shelter, the San Diego Humane Society, we have more than 1,500 animals in need of homes every single day. And that's in just one city! So what can you do to help them?

Here are a few ways you can make a difference:

Mocha
Page 54

1. Ask for a **humane education class** at your school. These classes are a terrific way to start getting involved in making the world a better place for animals.

2. **Be an ambassador!** Bring home all the knowledge you learn about how to take great care of animals. Let your parents, siblings, and all your friends and relatives know how important it is to respect and care for animals properly.

3. Write your local **legislators** about an animal issue you learned about or experienced firsthand. Our government officials are here to help and want to hear your ideas to make the world a better place.

4. Go meet the staff at your **local animal shelter.** Many shelters have humane education classes or camps and programs you can enroll in. Some will even bring these classes to you at your school as a special event.

5. Hold your own **animal rescue event.** You can hold a bake sale, organize a car wash, collect donations of pet food and supplies at school, or use a birthday party to ask for donations instead of gifts. (Believe me, you'll be plenty rewarded when you see all the good your donation will do!)

6. **Volunteer** at your local shelter. From walking dogs to brushing and reading to cats, all of these jobs are vital to help shelter animals have a happier time while they wait for their new homes. You may need to bring a parent along with you.

7. Be an **advocate for spaying and neutering** your pets. Let the whole world know that this is the number one, most important thing you can do to decrease the numbers of homeless animals all over the country.

8. Always look out for the safety of animals, whether they are pets, livestock, or wildlife. All animals rely on us for **protection.** So if you see a dog who looks lonely chained up to his doghouse, ask your parents about it. If you find a bird outside who can't fly, get some help to bring him to your local veterinarian, animal shelter, or wildlife rehabilitation facility.

9. Skip a visit to circuses, animal theme parks where animals can't roam freely, or racetracks that use **animals for entertainment.** These animals are not having a good life and will never go home to the wild or pasture where they belong. A sanctuary is a different thing: Those animals have been rescued and are living the best lives they can now that they're not "working" for humans anymore.

10. Always **adopt or rescue** a pet if you can. There are some very good breeders out there who can get your family a specific breed of dog or cat and that's fine, but never buy a pet from a pet store or over the Internet. Chances are, those animals came from a puppy mill and we hope to close that kind of business down.

11. Meet your local **veterinarian.** If you love animals, maybe this is a career you'd like to learn more about. Most veterinarians love meeting kids in their community. Maybe you can share some of the knowledge you learned in your humane education class or at your local shelter!

In my 25 years working to protect animals, some of the most passionate, helpful, and lifesaving volunteers I've ever met have been kids! Even if you aren't able to adopt a pet right now, kids like you have the power to make the world a better place for all animals. Best of all, there are so many ways to help—from volunteering at shelters to starting fund-raisers to raising awareness right inside your own home. Try out some of these ideas, then start saving animals. You'll be a rescue ambassador!

HUMANE EDUCATION
WITH
DEBBIE DUEL

from the Humane Rescue Alliance

Read Nigel's story on page 103.

Kids are powerful people—

that's what humane educator Debbie Duel believes. She teaches kids about making kind, compassionate, and responsible decisions. Debbie (meet her rescue dog, Nigel, on page 103) encourages kids like you to be good to others—including animals—and to make a difference in the world. Debbie works at the Humane Rescue Alliance in Washington, D.C. That's an organization that serves more than 60,000 animals each year. Here, Debbie shares some of her thoughts about how kids can help homeless animals.

SPEAK UP FOR ANIMALS. If I talk to a class of 25 students and we talk about speaking up for animals, and if each of those students talks to one other person and shares the same information, we are doubling our ability to help animals. Our program is designed to encourage activism. That means using your voice to help animals. Not everyone can adopt an animal companion, but everyone can care and act on their concern.

KIDS CAN HELP. I get really excited when kids speak up about the important work that shelters do. It's a great way for kids to help. Speak up! Take a stand! Every action helps. Everyone can make a difference. Several years ago a Girl Scout troop created a flyer asking for pet food donations. They collected lots of food and treats for animals in shelters. They also let their neighbors know that shelters rely on community support. In another case, a local 4-H group collected toys, treats, and cash for the animals four years ago. Today their effort has morphed into a community-wide event that happens every year. The best projects, like these, are ones that help familiarize others with the plight of homeless animals.

ADOPT. Kids can help encourage people to adopt rather than purchase animals. Visit your local shelter and encourage others to do the same. It can save a life!

Index

109

Index

Credits

FRONT COVER: (dog), Ruth O'Leary/Ruthless Photos; (cat & dog), Jessica Jarjabka/Courtesy of Cleveland Animal Protective League; (horse), Sarah K Andrew on behalf of DEFHR; (pig), Edgar's Mission Inc; **SPINE:** deamles for sale/Shutterstock; **BACK COVER:** (cat), Burnell Yow!; (snake), Reptile Rescue Center; (dog), Lori Epstein/National Geographic Creative; (bunnies), Callie Broaddus/NG Staff; (cows), Hof Butenland

INTERIOR: 1, Tom Benitez/Orlando Sentinel/Getty Images; 2-3, AP Photo/Mike Groll; 4 (UP), Jill Hayes Photography; 4 (CTR), Hamilton the Hipster Cat; 4 (LO LE), Youssef Farouk Baker; 5 (UP), Puget Sound Goat Rescue; 5 (CTR), Eddy Rambo; 5 (LO), Hog Haven Farm; 6 (BOTH), Best Friends Animal Society; 7 (UP), Best Friends Animal Society/Kurt Budde; 7 (LO), Best Friends Animal Society/Sarah Kichas; 8 (UP), ASB; 8 (CTR), Edgar's Mission Inc; 8 (LO), Courtesy of Lil BUB; 9, Jeff Heimsath/NG Staff; 10-11, Alexandra Gomez; 12 (ALL), Jessica Jarjabka/Courtesy of Cleveland Animal Protective League; 13 (UP LE), Gregory Marcel; 13 (UP RT), Gregory Marcel; 13 (LO LE), Jennifer Swanson; 13 (LO RT), Martha Bouza, M.D.; 14 (ALL), Edgar's Mission Inc; 15 (UP), Jennifer Gray for Beagle Freedom Project; 15 (LO), Hamilton the Hipster Cat; 16 (BOTH), Youssef Farouk Baker; 17 (UP LE), Geoffrey Tischman Photography; 17 (UP RT), Geoffrey Tischman Photography; 17 (LO), Stephen Lemmons; 18 (UP), Julia Jazynka; 18 (LO), WENN/Newscom; 19 (BOTH), Jennifer Bashford; 20, Colleen Bogner; 21 (UP LE), Will Preslar; 21 (UP RT), Dirty Paw Photography/Sabrina Moore; 21 (CTR), Jason Bone; 21 (LO), Colleen Bogner; 22 (BOTH), Shirley Braha; 23 (UP), Onefivenine/Dreamstime; 23 (LO LE & LO RT), Kay Hyman/Charleston Animal Society; 24 (UP LE), Animal Alliance of New Jersey; 24 (UP RT), Kelley Peters; 24 (LO), Kelley Peters; 25 (UP LE), Hintau Aliaksei/Shutterstock; 25 (UP RT), cynoclub/Shutterstock; 25 (LO), Courtney Hunt; 26, Edgar's Mission Inc; 27 (UP), Tom Towler; 27 (LO), Marji Beach/Animal Place; 28 (UP), Charla Kingsley;

28 (LO), Jeff Witherow; 29 (BOTH), Carol Beyer; 30, Jason Scott; 31 (ALL), Jason Scott; 32, Jennifer Milner; 33 (UP), courtesy Amber arienthal; 33 (CTR LE), Roger Migdow; 33 (CTR RT), courtesy Amber Marienthal; 33 (LO), Jamie Toschi; 34 (BOTH), Alexandra Gomez; 35 (UP), Hof Butenland; 35 (LO), On the Wings of Angels Rescue; 36 (BOTH), Shawn Rocco/Duke Health; 37 (UP), Mark Thiessen/NG Staff; 37 (LO LE & LO RT), Kitson Jazynka; 38 (BOTH), ASB; 39 (UP), Sarah K Andrew on behalf of DEFHR; 39 (LO), Jill Hayes Photography; 40 (UP), John Del Pozzo; 40 (LO), Lilly Chapa; 41 (BOTH), Wales News Service Ltd.; 42 (UP), Anne Heaton-Lewis; 42 (LO), Collin County Animal Services; 43 (ALL), VarisiriM; 44-45 (BOTH), Alex DeForest/Arizona Humane Society; 46 (UP), Heather Gutshall; 46 (LO LE & LO RT), Shelby Alinsky; 47 (BOTH), Annette Traband; 48, Best Friends Animal Society/Molly Wald; 49 (UP), Best Friends Animal Society; 49 (LO), Best Friends Animal Society/Kurt Budde; 50, courtesy Ruby Ridpath; 51 (UP), Christian Shenouda Photography; 51 (LO), Aaron Colborn; 52 (UP), courtesy Animal Care Centers of NYC (ACC); 52 (LO), Jon Busdeker/Orlando Sentinel/Getty Images; 53 (UP), Allie Nambo; 53 (LO), Jordan Hamlett Sanders; 54, Callie Broaddus/NG Staff; 55 (UP), Jeff Heimsath/NG Staff; 55 (LO), Callie Broaddus/NG Staff; 56 (BOTH), Puget Sound Goat Rescue; 57 (UP), Pamela B. Townsend; 57 (LO), Sarah Coltrin; 58 (RT), Bettmann/Getty Images; 58 (LE), Smithsonian Institution, National Museum of American History; 59 (UP), courtesy Bill Wynne; 59 (LO), Topical Press Agency/Hulton Archive/Getty Images; 60 (UP), Callie Broaddus/NG Staff; 60 (LO), Sarah Dukti; 61 (UP), Amanda Collado; 61 (LO LE & LO RT), Carter Bowersox; 62 (ALL), Eddy Rambo; 63 (UP), Albert Pedroza/San Antonio Fire Department; 63 (LO LE & LO RT), VSCD/C. Haggerty; 64-65, Robert Dollwet; 66 (BOTH), C. Haggerty; 67 (UP), Burnell Yow!; 67 (CTR, LO LE & LO RT), Reptile Rescue Center; 68 (UP), Christian Shenouda Photography; 68 (LO), The Labs & Co; 69 (BOTH), Shelly Roche; 70 (BOTH),

Honey Bee: Blind Cat from Fiji; 71 (UP), Lexie Boezeman Cataldo/In Joy Photography; 71 (LO), Linda Hickey; 72 (BOTH), Cherie Helman; 73 (UP LE & UP RT), DEFHR; 73 (LO), Steve Winter (Panthera);74 (UP), Elisabeth Smith; 74 (CTR), Sara Kenigsberg/Getty Images; 74 (LO), Terry Cummings; 75 (UP), Shelley McCammon; 75 (LO), courtesy Elizabeth Ober; 76 (BOTH), Aline Newman; 77 (UP), Whitney Hanson/Humane Society of North Texas; 77 (LO), Cynoclub/Dreamstime; 78 (RT), Keelie Mapp; 78 (LE), Eric Isselée/Shutterstock; 79 (UP), DEFHR; 79 (LO), Danielle Kiemel/Getty Images; 80-81 (ALL), AP Photo/Mike Groll; 82 (UP LE & UP RT), Bill Jordan; 82 (LO), Bayview Retirement Community; 83 (UP), Cindy Cribbs; 83 (LO), K. Avenson Photography; 84 (UP), Animal Aid Unlimited; 84 (LO), Lisa Bosley/NG Staff; 85 (BOTH), Derek Fowles Photography; 86 (UP LE), Eleanor Garrett; 86 (UP RT), Jennifer Karakul; 86 (LO), Grant Melton; 87 (UP LE), Rudi Taylor; 87 (UP RT), Tibrina Hobson/Getty Images for American Humane Association; 87 (LO), Rudi Taylor; 88 (UP), Christopher Peterson/Splash News; 88 (CTR & LO), Jill Cooper/Friendship Animal Protective League; 89, Sherri Earman; 90 (UP), Ed Van Buren; 90 (CTR & LO), Gentle Carousel Miniature Therapy Horses; 91 (ALL), Caroline Hagedorn; 92-93, Ruth O'Leary/Ruthless Photos; 94, Edgar's Mission Inc; 95 (UP), Vicky Vinch; 95 (LO), Hog Haven Farm; 96, Edgar's Mission Inc; 97 (UP & CTR), Ross Parry; 97 (LO), Roger Triantafilo; 98 (BOTH), Courtesy of Lil BUB; 99 (UP LE), Courtney Dasher; 99 (UP RT), Courtney Dasher; 99 (LO), San Gabriel Valley Humane Society; 100 (BOTH), Caters News Agency; 101 (UP), Jennifer Bertsch; 101 (LO), Lori Esptein/Nat Geo Creative; 102 (UP LE), Jennifer Kluesner; 102 (UP RT), Jennifer Kluesner; 102 (LO), Leeboo Photography; 103 (UP), Pamela B. Townsend; 103 (LO), Debra Duel; 104-105, Caroline Kraus; 106 (UP), Wales News Service; 106 (LO), courtesy Gary Weitzman; 107, Michelle Tyler/NG Staff; 108, Max Perez-Duel; 112, Best Friends Animal Society/Kurt Budde

Since 1888, the National Geographic Society has funded more than 12,000 research, exploration, and preservation projects around the world. The Society receives funds from National Geographic Partners, LLC, funded in part by your purchase. A portion of the proceeds from this book supports this vital work. To learn more, visit natgeo.com/info.

For more information, visit nationalgeographic.com, call 1-800-647-5463, or write to the following address:
National Geographic Partners
1145 17th Street N.W.
Washington, D.C. 20036-4688 U.S.A.

Visit us online at nationalgeographic.com/books

For librarians and teachers: ngchildrensbooks.org

More for kids from National Geographic:
kids.nationalgeographic.com

For information about special discounts for bulk purchases, please contact National Geographic Books Special Sales: specialsales@natgeo.com

For rights or permissions inquiries, please contact National Geographic Books Subsidiary Rights: bookrights@natgeo.com

Art directed by Sanjida Rashid
Designed by Simon Renwick

Library of Congress Cataloging-in-Publication Data

Title: 125 pet rescues : from pound to palace : homeless pets made happy / by National Geographic Kids.
Other titles: One hundred twenty-five pet rescues | National Geographic kids.
Description: Washington, D.C. : National Geographic Kids, 2017. | Includes index.
Identifiers: LCCN 2016030511| ISBN 9781426327360 (pbk. : alk. paper) | ISBN 9781426327377 (library binding : alk. paper)
Subjects: LCSH: Pet adoption—Juvenile literature. | Animal shelters—Juvenile literature. | Animal rescue—Juvenile literature.
Classification: LCC SF416.2 .A16 2017 | DDC 636.088/7--dc23
LC record available at https://lccn.loc.gov/2016030511

Printed in China
17/RRDS/1

The publisher would like to thank: Kitson Jazynka, author; Aline Alexander Newman and Nancy Furstinger, contributing writers; Simon Renwick, designer; Paige Towler, project editor; Sanjida Rashid, art director; Lori Epstein, photo director; Kelley Miller, photo editor; Jennifer Geddes, fact-checker; Alix Inchausti, production editor; Best Friends Animal Society, for their continued devotion to animals in need; Dr. Gary Weitzman, for his commitment to animal welfare; and Debbie Duel, for her tireless advocacy.

Roosevelt
Page 49